Wolf Whistle
Politics

Wolf Whistle Politics

The New Misogyny in America Today

Edited by
Diane Wachtell

Introduction by
Dr. Naomi Wolf

THE NEW PRESS

25 YEARS

NEW YORK
LONDON

Requests for permission to reproduce selections from this book should be mailed to:
Permissions Department, The New Press,
120 Wall Street, 31st floor, New York, NY 10005.

Published in the United States by The New Press, New York, 2017
Distributed by Perseus Distribution

ISBN 978-1-62097-352-3 (pb)
ISBN 978-1-62097-353-0 (e-book)
CIP data is available

The New Press publishes books that promote and enrich public discussion and
understanding of the issues vital to our democracy and to a more equitable world.
These books are made possible by the enthusiasm of our readers; the support
of a committed group of donors, large and small; the collaboration of our many
partners in the independent media and the not-for-profit sector; booksellers, who
often hand-sell New Press books; librarians; and above all by our authors.

www.thenewpress.com

Book design and composition by dix!
This book was set in Electra

Printed in the United States of America

2   4   6   8   10   9   7   5   3   1

Contents

Introduction by Dr. Naomi Wolf   ix

Wolf Whistle Politics: Taking Back the
Conversation to Advance Women's Rights   xvii
Wendy Davis

Part I: Presidential Politics

The Woman Card   3
Jill Lepore

The Woman's Party   17
Namara Smith

Which Women Support Hillary (and Which Women
Can't Afford To)   29
Sarah Leonard

Black Feminists Don't Owe Hillary Clinton Their Support   35
Kirsten West Savali

Feminism at the Polls   41
Liza Featherstone

Don't Call Clinton a Weak Candidate:
It Took Decades of Scheming to Beat Her   49
Rebecca Solnit

Part II: Sexism and Misogyny

Donald and Billy on the Bus   55
Lindy West

At Least Six Women Have Accused Trump
of Sexual Misconduct—How Many More Will
Come Forward?   59
Joan Walsh

Why We Trust Donald Trump's Accusers but
Didn't Believe Bill Clinton's   63
Caitlin Flanagan

Hillary Clinton Has One More Badly Behaved Man
Left to Vanquish   67
Katha Pollitt

Part III: Women and Governance

What Wendy Davis Stood For   73
Amy Davidson

How Can We Get More Women in Elected Office?
Look to New Hampshire   75
Rebecca Hellmich

Women Actually Do Govern Differently   81
Claire Miller

The Senate Bathroom Angle   85
Gail Collins

Part IV: Moving Forward

The Men Feminists Left Behind   91
Jill Filipovic

An Open Letter to White Liberal Feminists   97
LeRhonda Manigault-Bryant

Identity Issues Don't Distract from Economic Issues —
They Are Economic Issues   101
Rebecca Traister

Political Correctness: How the Right Invented
a Phantom Enemy   105
Moira Weigel

Part V: What Happens Next?

Feminism Lost. Now What?   123
Susan Chira

You Never Know What a Revolution Is Going to Look Like   129
Naomi Wolf

Thirteen Women Who Should Run in 2020   133
Amy Davidson

How a Fractious Women's Movement Came to Lead the Left   139
Amanda Hess

Sexist Political Criticism Finds a New Target:
Kellyanne Conway   155
Susan Chira

Introduction

Dr. Naomi Wolf

Dr. Naomi Wolf is the author of eight bestselling nonfiction books, including The Beauty Myth *and* Vagina: A New Biography. *She recently earned a doctorate from the University of Oxford. A former Gore advisor, Wolf is CEO of DailyClout, a media company that makes tech tools and content for democracy, and the author of the forthcoming* Outrages.

When I published a book called *Vagina* four years ago, arguing that targeting the genitals and sexuality of women was a political ploy, and that women needed to defend their sexuality—and even their genitals—overtly in order to be a potent political force, the topic was seen to be outré, and I was chastised for introducing women's reproductive organs into politics. The vagina has since made many rather shocking appearances in the political fray. Donald Trump and Billy Bush talked about grabbing women's vaginas without permission. The *New York Times* ran the word "pussy" on the front page for the first time in its history. And when a woman with a national platform— Fox News's Megyn Kelly—called Donald Trump out on broadcast television, like a metronome, Trump invoked for viewers the image of Ms. Kelly's bleeding vagina. This attack was meant to silence Kelly, as attacks on women's vaginas—indeed the mere invocation of that shameful, silencing term—always have been.

But on the Mall in Washington the day after Donald Trump's inauguration, you couldn't shut nearly a half million women up about their genitals, their reproductive organs, and the politics of defending and attacking them. A groundswell of furious, mainstream-as-can-be women carried signs that were newly combative and explicit: "This Pussy Grabs Back" was one, and "If I wanted the government in my uterus, I'd fuck a congressman" was another. The icon of a uterus with fallopian tubes was on many signs; on one, the organ itself was giving Trump the finger. "You really like it? No, I really don't" was yet another.

In DC, New York, Seattle, London, New Delhi, and Christchurch, women—and the men who support them—flowed into a vast, iconic river of "pink pussyhats"—1.7 million of these were knitted by the Pussyhat Project and worn at protests around the country and the world. Women of every background and age showed up wearing an item symbolizing a very personal part of their bodies, screaming mad in defense of their genitals, their wombs, their vital organs. Sick of sexual abuse. Sick of loss of reproductive control. Sick of being degraded. They even brought their kids to the marches; today's rage was going to infect the next generation.

This huge response was a result, I believe, of women's awareness of a newly brutal form of political engagement, an overtly misogynist approach, aptly described by former Texas state senator Wendy Davis (of filibuster fame) in a speech she gave at Princeton in 2015 as "Wolf Whistle Politics."

What accounts for such explicit, in-your-face sexism at this moment in time? I would hazard that it's the prospect of women in power at last. The presidential race clearly inflamed this new brutality. But it was just tinder that has been ready for some time to set a bonfire ablaze. The year 2016 was the year in which gender issues exploded all over the American political map. Everywhere you looked there was evidence of a gender crisis: gendered hope and gendered hostility; gendered rage, violence, and fear; pussy grabbing and invocations of Seneca Falls.

Even in his manic, tantrum-y chaos, Candidate Trump inhabited the current moment in America in which men and women really live: our world of social media impulsivity, nonstop porn, shock jocks, celebrity worship, and raw emotional battle. He particularly called out to the serious divides between haves and have-nots, both male and female. It all erupted continually during the last presidential campaign in America, and the shards poked awkwardly—and at times painfully—through what had been the last fragile veneers of polite traditional political discourse.

The essays collected in this book assemble into a legible mosaic the many fragments of that eruption. Yes, of course, the presidential race was where most of the action was, but this volume pulls the lens back, broadening the discussion to include a wide range of women and issues in the openly bigoted and sexist public sphere today.

In her Princeton speech, Wendy Davis likened wolf whistle politics to the coded signaling of "dog whistle politics," which scholar Ian Haney Lopez used to characterize racist political pandering, as exemplified by Richard Nixon's infamous Southern strategy. But where dog whistling is covert and happens at a pitch that can't be heard by many, wolf whistling is right there in your face. Wolf whistling is an undisguised lasciviousness that condones and informs, Davis asserts, "the sexualized nature in which women candidates and women's issues are often framed." Women candidates, as Davis notes, are viciously and openly sexualized with impunity. She talks about how she was targeted with sexualized imagery to demean her during her senatorial bid. As she points out, "the ploy works, so why stop?"

At this moment in history, Davis's term can easily be expanded to include the play of overt and violent misogyny throughout public life, including women of all kinds: voters, marchers, spokeswomen, workers, medical patients, moms, and other everyday female leaders, political and not. Though the Trump/Clinton matchup in 2016 was the catalyst, like Betty Friedan's "problem that has no name" in the 1960s, and Susan Faludi's "backlash" in the 1990s, the concept of "wolf whistle politics" allows us to discern the contours of a contemporary constellation we may not have perceived before. If we trace the thread of vicious, angry, and sexualized sexism—as opposed to the more polite, condescending sexism of the first decade or so of the twenty-first century—we can use the concept of wolf whistle politics to smoke out and name a whole gamut of tactics that have somehow, appallingly, made their way back to America's center stage.

Today, my news feed shows President Trump signing an executive order limiting access to birth control and safe abortions in countries that receive US aid. He is flanked by seven white men with their hands folded nervously over their gray-suit-clad penises. The irony of the photo went viral.

Why are the vagina and the uterus the sites of such naked political battle right now? The retrograde, throwback nature of wolf whistle politics must be placed in the context of the history of the women's movement, which has always seen a one-step-back reaction to any steps forward. This last year has seen several steps forward, but the response has been a symbolic political gang rape down a dark alley. Many of us feel as if the current of history is suddenly flowing in reverse. Younger women may simply be stunned by it, but the frenzy of public sexism reminds those of us who are older of earlier days. Women who remember firsthand the violent hostility of the mid-1960s to early 1970s, when feminists were openly derided in the media as bitches, dykes (in a bad way), and harridans, say, "I can't believe I am here again—we are here again." As one midlife feminist put it, incredulously, "It feels like we are back on the barricades with Nora Ephron and Eleanor Holmes Norton."

Is it an accident that we keep referencing the stirrings of the last wave of feminism in pop culture? *Mad Men* ends just as the ladies have finally had it. Another hit series, *The Crown*, shows the most powerful woman in Britain, initially hobbled by gender norms of the 1950s, slowly awakening to demand an education and a real say. The Amazon Prime series *Good Girls Revolt* dramatizes the process of turning the tide of sexism at *Newsweek* in the 1960s.

During the current era of wolf whistle politics, fights that appeared to be over—Title IX protections and the basic fight that won *Roe v. Wade*, for instance—have been reawakened. State by state, laws have been passed to make abortions practically unattainable if you can't drive far, if you don't have a lot of money, or if you don't have child-care options for your family. The last election cycle also saw a red-in-tooth-and-claw attack on funding for Planned Parenthood—that staid, even mainstream organization that most Americans understood was there, no matter what, for your Pap smear or, quietly, no matter what you said in church, for your daughter's emergency Plan B. The ghosts of old dangers—of the horror stories of back alley abortions and the images of bloodied coat hangers—that terrified me as a child, when I leafed through my mother's *Ms.* magazine in the early 1970s, are haunting our homes and our dreams. And in a small but telling sign of the times, mere weeks after the election, Amazon canceled *Good Girls Revolt*, a step taken, as *The Atlantic* reported, "with no women . . . involved in the decision."

Exemplifying this return to an earlier era is the use of the term "locker room talk" to excuse and legitimize the sexual demeaning, domination, and abuse of women. The term was deployed by Donald Trump to explain away the infamous "pussy grab" video, in which Trump shared his penchant for what is legally defined as sexual assault. And the phrase gave cover to Billy Bush, when he sought to normalize his predator-enabling behavior by invoking that time-honored, all-male space "the locker room." As if, somehow, attitudes and propensities acknowledged out of earshot don't inform actual conduct with actual women. Many athletes signed a letter vociferously objecting to this "guys will be guys" view of sexual violence, and men of all backgrounds publicly disavowed such attitudes. But had guys changed? How many guys had changed? Did that lightning-rod moment mean that, while some guys held tight to old and savage gender privileges, thousands, or millions, of others were done with them? Only near-term history will show if patriarchy is finally tired of itself.

The uterus has made other dramatic appearances in politics recently. Mike Pence was breathtakingly candid during the vice presidential debate about his view that women should not control their own reproductive rights. And women are coming forward again, as they last did in the 1970s, to speak out about their own abortions.

The penis has made dramatic political appearances as well. Anthony Weiner's snaps of his genitals on social media became a powerful opposition tool for Republicans. Missteps—even serious missteps—by powerful white men, whose errant sexuality in the past was politely glossed over by other white men, became lurid fodder for political battle. Anthony Weiner's penis was used as a way to attack both his wife, Huma Abedin, and Secretary Clinton, replaying traditional uses of the phallus to smite powerful women.

Other important fragmenting points in the drama of wolf whistle politics were caused by how diverse kinds of women reacted to the same instigations. Many white women voters countenanced or explained away Trump's predatory proclivities in ways that other white women couldn't fathom. Class, region, race, and age were all dividers—the debate between Maggie Hassan and Kelly Ayotte in New Hampshire over whether Trump was a good role model for kids showed political divides about appropriate male behavior—all women were obviously not the same. Today in my social media feed, a video of a furious African American woman at the march, with a sign about the erasure of race, was backed by three ditsy-looking white women in pink pussy hats taking selfies, exemplifying the tensions between women of color and white women in a female-hostile political season.

Michelle Obama versus Kellyanne Conway. Loretta Lynch, Samantha Power, Alicia Garza, Eve Ensler. In the face of raging misogyny, everyone deployed "their" women. This moment made clear that there is no one feminism and no single way of addressing male misbehavior.

By summer 2016, we were witnessing a flat-out gender war in the national US psyche—one that took some of us back to memories of Bobby Riggs versus Billie Jean King in a different kind of competition. It seemed as if the looming prospect of a potential shoo-in first woman president—heiress to the well-heeled Clinton legacy and political machine, former secretary of state, darling of power brokers on both sides of the aisle—had raised, with fairy-tale logic, its oppositional id: the walking, vengeful phallus.

Was Secretary Clinton issuing noble-sounding sound bites urging people to "Stand with Me"? There was Mr. Trump, with his inflamed face and ever-bouffant hair, serving as a mouthpiece for the male resistance to this specter of ultimate female empowerment. Did Secretary Clinton present an image of a woman giving a leader-of-the-free-world-type speech? There was Candidate Trump, directing attention continually to what was gross, demeaning, or objectifying about women's bodies, calling even beauty pageant winners "fat pigs" and "eating machines." Trump commanded the power of male judgment of female physicality, exercising one of the last privileges standing of a fading, furious patriarchy. As Secretary Clinton paced about in her overly polished candidate's manner, asking us to imagine her in the Oval Office, all Trump had to do was stalk behind her and stand there, looming.

The essays in this book showcase the many moments when wolf whistle politics were at play—not just in the presidential election, but over the last few years of our common life. They also provide the historical backdrop of women in American politics over a longer arc. Jill Lepore fills in the much-needed history of the women's vote, explicating Secretary Clinton's reference in her nomination victory speech to the first women's rights convention in 1848 in Seneca Falls and more. Other contributors shine a light on the racial and class issues that were part of the violence of this presidential race and this larger historical moment. Namara Smith's "The Woman's Party" questions Clinton's abandonment of women who rely on welfare as a neoliberal shift away from the grassroots, particularly Clinton's belief that "what's best for the market is best for women." This, Smith rightly notes, lost Clinton the support of younger women in the primaries. Sarah Leonard, in her influential essay "Which Women Support Hillary (and Which Women Can't Afford To)," takes this class-based critique further, calling the former candidate "an enemy of the poor." Race is addressed in ways the mainstream media never bothered to investigate during the election, with withering contributions from Kirsten West Savali, Yasmin Nair, and LeRhonda Manigault-Bryant. Well-known Clinton critics, like Liza Featherstone, are paired with well-known Clinton supporters, like Rebecca Solnit.

Some of the most powerful takeaways in this collection come from the big-picture analyses of chaotic gender war. Claire Miller offers a study of decades of legislation, showing that women leaders do govern "differently" and are more likely than men to support bills around civil rights, health care, and education. In a useful glance into the future, Amy Davidson walks us through the bios of thirteen women candidates who are ready for 2020, poised to walk into what will no doubt be the even more dramatic and combative wolf whistle politics of the near future.

The essays that follow offer smoking-hot insights that together trace a new thing in American public life: naked primal political rage howling at women, in filthy and scary ways, in the twenty-first century.

And, it must be said: women howling back. One of the signs I loved at the march was that of my daughter's twenty-one-year-old friend, which read, simply, "I am so mad."

What will happen next? Put on your protective armor, in the form of some insight offered here, and enter this dangerous, inescapable fray.

Dr. Naomi Wolf, New York City, January 17, 2017

Wolf Whistle Politics:
Taking Back the Conversation
to Advance Women's Rights

Wendy Davis

Wendy Russell Davis is an American lawyer and Democratic politician from Fort Worth, Texas. Davis represented District 10 in the Texas Senate from 2009 to 2015 and, in 2013, held an eleven-hour-long filibuster to block more restrictive abortion regulations for Texas. She delivered the speech "Wolf Whistle Politics: Taking Back the Conversation to Advance Women's Rights" to Princeton's Woodrow Wilson College in February 2015.

This is my first time to speak publicly since my gubernatorial candidacy, and I'm very excited to be "back in the saddle," as we would say in Texas. I am here today to address gender, specifically why gender equality is losing ground and how we can work to reverse that. I'm going to ask you to challenge conventional thinking regarding how we define and talk about gender equality, and I'll hopefully help you understand the lens through which I view these issues a bit better. More and more I'm coming to understand and appreciate how much our individual filters matter, especially in the way we approach conversations in the political framework. I would like to invite us to consider each other's personal perspectives, each other's lenses, as we strive to move women's equality forward.

I was eleven when my parents divorced, and my ninth-grade-educated mother, who had never been in the workforce before, was left to financially support four children on her own while my father pursued his dream of starting a nonprofit theater. We were thrown from a blue-collar lifestyle into poverty almost overnight. Watching my mother struggle to put food on the table from a low-wage fast-food restaurant job made me want more for myself—made me want to ensure that I would never be left without an education and the means to support myself. And yet, I too fell in that well of poverty for a time. Pregnant at eighteen and married for a very brief time, at nineteen I was left to support myself and my infant daughter, Amber. With only one semester of college under my belt, I could not have been prepared for what looked like a very long, bleak road ahead. My greatest fear was coming true. I was going to live the same struggles that I had watched my mother live. Fear can be a powerful motivator. My fears were reinforced on nights when I would come home to find my electricity had been shut off, or when I had to experience the embarrassment of choosing items to put back as I stood in the grocery store line because I didn't have enough money for that week's food.

But I'm here today because policies that support a woman's ability to climb out of a deep well of poverty actually do work. These policies, and the legislation that support them, are not, as some of my former legislative colleagues in Texas believe, handouts. Instead, they are ladders—much-needed avenues for those who have found themselves in a hole, in large part, simply because they are women. My ladders came in several forms.

One was access to an affordable community college education with grants and low-cost tuition that even I could afford, which ultimately was my gateway to graduating from Harvard Law School ten years later. Another ladder, for me, came in the form of access to reproductive and Well-Woman health care that I received from the Planned Parenthood clinic near my home. For several years, as an uninsured woman, that clinic was my only source of care. It was the place where I received cancer screenings, blood tests for diabetes, and Well-Woman exams. But, most importantly, it was the place that provided me with the ability to control my reproductive destiny, so that once I put my foot on the path to higher education I could be assured of keeping it there. Another ladder came in the form of childcare and the transportation needed to access it: I was fortunate that I had a friend who was willing to sit my young daughter, Amber, and to charge me a reasonable amount for it. I was also fortunate that I had a car. I had the means of transportation to get Amber to childcare and get myself to work and school. For many women who are trying to climb the ladder from poverty to stability today, inaccessibility to childcare and transportation are sufficient roadblocks to hold them down. For this very reason, I was pleased to hear President Obama talk about access to quality childcare as part of his focus in his recent State of the Union Address.

I was struck, in my legislative experience, by a young woman who came and spoke to our Senate Education Committee. She was seventeen years old. She was speaking on behalf of a dropout recovery school that she was attending. She had a child when she was fifteen, and she thought the possibility of graduating from high school did not exist for her. When she wanted to give up, the school came and found her. When it got too hard to take the bus to day care to drop off her child and then take another bus to go to school, when she wanted to give up, this school would not let her fail. They wouldn't let her fall through the cracks. Programs like that are helping to make sure that women can realize their dreams. Understanding her story and the challenges that are created for young women like her, who are struggling to find quality childcare and transportation so that they can access education to improve themselves, should be a reminder how important policies like that are.

Finally, one of my ladders came from the good fortune of working for an employer who allowed me flexible working hours so I could attend classes at community college. Good workplace policies like that could make this environment possible for more women who are where I once was. Those years were a tremendous struggle and they were filled with fear. But I am grateful for the motivation that fear provided and so very grateful for the lens the struggle provided me. There are so many women today who cannot tell the same story that I have the blessed ability to stand before you to tell. The ladder-climbing support—affordable college tuition, reproductive health care, quality childcare, transportation, flexible work hours—is not there for them, as those things once were for me. We find ourselves fighting old fights and in many instances losing ground, but why? Quite simply, because women's reproductive rights and other issues important to women's equality have been hijacked by a far-right agenda that uses those issues as a wedge, a means to an end: to hold on to and further their political positions, status, and power. For these politicians, wielding women's issues as their tool to provoke favorable voting responses is much more important to them than the fallout that they leave behind.

To better explain my point I'll ask you to consider the argument made by Ian Haney Lopez in his book *Dog Whistle Politics*. Professor Lopez invites us to consider how coded, racial appeals have played a role in politics, often resulting in the middle class voting against its own economic interests. For voters, these racial appeals align with perceived social threats, which are far greater motivators. Lopez asserts that politicians employ techniques that play upon racial animus to get voters to react in ways that are favorable to a politician's desire to obtain or maintain political power.

To demonstrate his point, Lopez traces accounts of presidential candidates using racial dog whistling to elicit voter support—candidates like George Wallace, who was at first ridiculed as an unrepentant redneck because he was so extreme in verbalizing his support for blatantly racist policies. He openly defended segregation and proudly extolled the Anglo-Saxon Southland, but even Wallace learned that this was not something helpful to him. Instead he learned that by using less racially charged language, he could still invite race-based voter responses without crossing the line and alienating those voters who did not respond well to overt racism. Wallace stopped talking about objections to desegregation itself, and, instead, started talking about states' rights to turn away "arrogant federal authority." (That language ought to sound familiar to us today. Consider some of the ways in which the opposition to the Affordable Care Act or immigration reform are voiced in today's political environment.) In so doing, Wallace found that he was on to something: the ability to mobilize voters based on racial animus and racial fears without ever having to mention race. His softened language gave those who opposed racial integration permission to exercise racially motivated electoral responses without having to admit to others, or even to themselves, their racial bias.

Barry Goldwater too talked of his support for states' rights and freedom of association, bragging about his vote against the Civil Rights

Act when he ran for president in 1964. And Richard Nixon, who employed the now politically infamous Southern strategy to motivate votes in the South, used coded dog whistle language against "forced busing" to engender racial animus and court votes from those who felt threatened by the desegregation of public schools. Even Democrats are guilty of using this ploy. President Jimmy Carter, pointing out that he did not support the forced integration of cultural communities, was dog whistling to voters who objected to federal policies integrating low-income, mostly minority housing into non-low-income, non-minority communities. So was Ronald Reagan when he described the young buck behind you in the grocery store line buying sirloin steak with food stamps while you were buying hamburger meat with your hard-earned paycheck. Each of these was a strategic use of race to gain votes. Importantly, Professor Lopez points out that this strategic use of race stands apart from other forms of racism, because the driving force behind strategic racism is not racial animus for its own sake, but rather—and perhaps more perniciously—to successfully pursue money, power, or status.

I saw this in my own gubernatorial race last year, when my opponent played upon fears regarding an invasion of illegal immigrants into Texas, calling openly for militarization of Texas border communities through support of the National Guard, even though those communities are some of the safest in our state—El Paso having been designated the safest large city in the country for the last four years running. Married to a Latina, Greg Abbott, my opponent, would hardly fit the typical definition of someone with racial animus toward Latinos, yet he understood how to dog whistle in a way that would inflame voters' perceived threats of a Latino invasion to better garner votes. But my opponent's dog whistling, like so many political candidates from the right, was not limited to provoking and playing upon perceived threats based on race. He, and others, also successfully employ the same kind of tactics to provoke votes based on gender biases and fears.

So, let's discuss the use of gender in that regard. Perhaps given the sexualized nature in which women candidates and women's issues are often framed, "wolf whistling," rather than dog whistling, might be a more apt way of describing this tactic. Some of that wolf whistling occurs in fairly blatant ways. For example, in my race, my opponent's supporters derided me by using photoshopped sexual images of me in social media, with my face or head on a very sexy body, inviting a response from potential voters to view me as a highly sexualized, rather than intelligent and confident, potential state leader.

There were also questions raised about my bona fides as a mother, with suggestions that I abandoned my children to attend law school. In so doing, attention was diverted from my achievements. I was no longer to be applauded for graduating law school while also juggling the responsibilities of caring for my young family. I was to be reviled for self-improvement at the expense of giving anything other than full-time attention to child rearing. And, of course, there were the abortion-Barbie postings on social media, and the posters put up around LA, when I attended a fund-raiser there, depicting my head atop a very sexy Barbie doll with a plastic baby doll in her uterus and a pair of scissors in my hand. These were images and critiques meant to invite others to believe that I should be viewed not as a potential state leader but as a sexualized woman and a traitor to traditional roles of women.

This was as strategic as it was flagrant. I'm not the first female candidate to experience it, and I certainly will not be the last. The ploy works, so why stop? These flagrant messages are supported by much more subtler ones also meant to provoke gender animus. Consider the number of politicians who use abortion as a political bogeyman. Certainly, some of this is meant to elicit a response from voters who are motivated by religious or moral ideas about the sanctity of life and their objections to pro-choice candidates on those terms. But there is something much less obvious, but no less powerful, at play as well: making abortion a central issue in the political arena also plays upon traditional patriarchal notions of a woman's role in society and invites voters to view abortion as an issue that threatens that role.

It is arguably understandable to see how playing on patriarchal sympathies would provoke favorable voting responses from some men. Abortion and other reproductive rights provide women with the autonomy to remain—and rise—in the workplace, creating competition for them and perhaps threatening their views of what they believe appropriate male-female roles should be. This perspective is one that is deeply rooted, whether consciously or unconsciously, and is a consequence of the notion that women ought to serve in traditional female roles: wife, stay-at-home mother, and supporter of her hunting and gathering man. But these perceived threats are not limited to those experienced by some men. Women too respond to whistling that invites them to feel threatened. Some women feel that their chosen role as stay-at-home wives and mothers will be devalued vis-à-vis sexually autonomous women, who exercise the choice to stall or abandon their reproductive role to rise in the workplace or the political arena. The conservative movement invites this response, invoking images of strong families and appropriate gender relations. Serving as the backdrop to this game are notions of punishment as well. Women who have sex and become pregnant should bear the brunt of their sexuality. They should live with the consequences.

Employing these tools, the far right proposes to be guarding the appropriate and noble role of women as homemakers, mothers, and caretakers. By inviting a negative response to gender-coded whistles, they play upon the notion that some hold, namely, that sex for women is supposed to be about procreation and motherhood only. A narrative that says otherwise, that argues in favor of access to contraception and other reproductive care, such as abortion, allows women to enjoy sex purely for the sake of sexual pleasure, and threatens concepts of traditional family values. In this context, conversations about contraception and abortion become a strategic means to an end, provoking fear-based responses in voters, who then feel threatened and resent this attempted disruption to their perceived world order and their place in it. Consider Rush Limbaugh's portrayal of Sandra Fluke as a slut when she advocated for mandatory inclusion of contraceptive care in healthcare plans. This whistling, provocatively and purposively, invoked responses from listeners, who perceived Ms. Fluke's position as one that would threaten their patriarchal notions of a woman's appropriate role. Guided by the moral framework expressed by Limbaugh, and others, wolf-whistlers invite listeners and voters to react to their own implicit fears that it is wrong, indeed immoral, for women to enjoy sex for reasons other than procreation.

Dr. Kristin Luker, a sociologist and professor at UC Berkeley, has written extensively on this topic. On abortion politics, she argues that the right-to-life movement represents an attempt not just to protect the fetus but to ensure that family is a higher priority among women than having a career—that women who choose to stay home are not relegated to a place of lower prestige relative to women who work outside the home. Taking her argument one step further, I believe it is the case that politicians are using the right-to-life movement, specifically, to engender fear in voters that woman's prestige in the home most certainly would suffer a blow were voters not to respond at the ballot box against pro-choice candidates. The whistlers don't even necessarily have to believe their own message. Many of them likely do not, but just as race-based dog whistling is often nothing more than the strategic means to an end, so too is the case with gender-based whistling. Tragically though, women's access to reproductive health care gets caught in the crossfire and becomes more and more threatened. Women's health—and indeed their lives—become collateral damage to a political scheme. So, how do we respond?

If my story is any kind of example, we'd make the argument that is often heard: supporting women to economic autonomy is good for the overall economy. Ensuring that women have access to education, health care, quality childcare, family leave—all of these things create an opportunity for women to be more successful, to have increased buying power in the economy, and that is good for the economic well-being of us all. This is the "when we all do better, we all do better" argument. It was the story that I told you at the beginning of my remarks about me, but that message isn't working to motivate voters. Why? Because it misses the point. It isn't speaking to the motives behind many voters' choices. It's a response that hasn't stopped first to look through the lens from which these voters are making their decisions.

Just think about the state of affairs that exists after the 2014 congressional elections. We now have a House and a Senate comprised of a majority of members who proudly articulate their desire to deregulate big business, to return to a laissez-faire approach that allows major polluters and multibillion-dollar corporations free rein and an even greater opportunity to grow their wealth disproportionately to most of the country's population, leaving the middle class to shoulder more and more of a tax burden. There was a time, post the Great Depression, when it would have been thought impossible that Americans would vote for candidates who would so willingly boast that they support the interests of the mega-wealthy against the interests of most of us. But American voters are voting for these candidates. The answer as to why lies, sadly, in the fact that an appeal has been made to something deeper inside them—something that trumps their economic concerns. These voters have allowed fears of societal threats to become their primary motivators at the ballot box. We see this with race. Look no further than the current conversation about immigration. We see this with gender. Legislation is either passing or percolating in states throughout this country, even in Congress, that employs the use of abortion as a political message and means to an end.

Arguing that creating a path to citizenship would be good for the economy, or that empowering women with reproductive autonomy is, likewise, good for the economy, is not going to get us far—as experience has shown us. Instead, we have to find a way to calm the fears that are being manufactured and manipulated. In the arena of gender, we might start by asking ourselves why so many young women are eschewing the term "feminism" today, buying into the right-wing message that tells them that standing for the feminist agenda—equal pay, reproductive rights, et cetera—will require them to check their femininity, their womanhood, at the door. Consider the kerfuffle that occurred a couple of months ago when, in an interview with *Redbook* magazine, twenty-nine-year-old Kaley Cuoco, female lead in the popular show *The Big Bang Theory*, declined to answer in the affirmative when she was asked whether she was a feminist. She asked, "Is it okay if I say no?" She said that she enjoyed cooking for her husband and that it makes her feel like a housewife, which she said she loved. She said, "It might sound old-fashioned, but I like the idea of women taking care of their men." Sadly, messaging from the far right has convinced her and so many other young women that feminism is about trading in their license to be women, to be feminine.

What we have to help her—and other young women—understand is that fighting for women's equality isn't about telling women how they have to live, or that they can't enjoy doing things that are considered traditionally female. Instead, it's about having the ability to choose freely what our roles will be. It is about being respected, regardless of what those choices look like. It is about the working woman celebrating and respecting her sister, who made a choice to stay home and care for her children full-time. It's about the stay-at-home mom cheering on the women who are putting those cracks in the glass ceiling. It's about each of us—as women and the men who love us—caring enough about each other to silence the noise that attempts to keep us at odds—noise that relishes in the fact that we feel we should be at odds with each other to feel less threatened by each other's individual choices. We have to create an inclusive and shared community that sends a message that we are all in this together. We must work to minimize—or do away with—perceived threats, flowing from the idea of embracing gender equality. We have to fight for an America where all choices made by women are respected and valued.

A *New York Times* article about me, during my gubernatorial race, ran under the cover-line "Can Wendy Davis Have It All?" Would we ever see this question asked about a male candidate? The better question is asked by Anne-Marie Slaughter, your Professor Emerita of Politics and International Affairs here at Princeton. In her TED Talk, she asks, "Can We All Have It All?" Presenting the idea that only when men can freely make choices about their role as breadwinner or stay-at-home husbands and fathers will we achieve true gender equality. She invites us to consider the importance of creating a world in which we equally celebrate either choice men and women make. True gender equality will come when we take care not to view each other's choices through a pejorative lens. We've got to trade eyeglasses and look through each other's filters, working our way to a place free of hostility or fear because we see that we cannot be our best selves without each other's support. We must humanize experiences in a way that makes them translatable and relatable.

I firmly believe that no one, whether they have an "R" or a "D" next to their name in a political context, wants the harmful, secondary impacts that have flowed from the war against Planned Parenthood and the closure of women's clinics that it has occasioned. In Texas alone, an estimated 180,000 women lost the only health care they had. They lost with it their access to contraceptive care and cancer screenings. This all came about through strategic defunding aimed at bludgeoning Planned Parenthood. The far right has done the political calculus. They know that making Planned Parenthood the bogeyman gets them votes. We should talk about the human casualties of this fight. We must invite each other, regardless of our perspective on choice, to care about the individuals who are impacted, whose health is put at risk—to talk about the women who will quite literally lose their lives because of maneuverings that have placed politics above people.

On the very top of the Texas capitol stands a statue, and it is not of a galloping cowboy or of a soldier protecting his land. It is of a woman. In her right hand she holds a lowered sword, and in her left hand she raises a lone star proudly above her. She is called "Goddess of Liberty." Porcelain white, her eyes are large and they reflect a steely resolve. Late at night, you can look up at the Goddess of Liberty and see her illuminated high atop the capitol dome. If you look closely during warm summer months, you can see the nighthawks diving and swirling around her, their small beaks and flatheads taking advantage of the glowing light surrounding the goddess to hunt for flying insects on a moonlit night. Through the wind and rain and brutal Texas heat, the Goddess of Liberty continues to stand. She stands for freedom and wisdom and justice. She is a symbol of everything that I was fighting for on that day in June of 2013, when I stood for almost thirteen hours: freedom and justice for women, and the wisdom of lawmakers to stop making women's bodies pawns in their political games. Appropriately and beautifully, it wasn't me alone who successfully carried that filibuster over the midnight deadline. It was the thousands of people, women and men, who were there, who had their own personal experiences they wanted to share, who had listened as I read the heart-wrenching stories of so many women and their families on the senate floor that day. There they were, demanding to be heard.

When their voices were artificially silenced through the parliamentary maneuverings that occurred that day, they rose, like the Goddess of Liberty—with that lone star raised above her head—they stood for something, for themselves, for each other, for women they have never met—nor will ever know—and, for at least a moment, they understood their own power. That power is in each of us. The power to stand, the power to unite with each other toward the common cause of seeing and understanding each other, bound by our shared human experiences of joy and triumph, failure and sorrow. Let's own that power, and let's use it to say, "I stand for a woman's right to choose freely the role that she will play, and I will fight for the tools that will provide her with that choice. And when she does choose, whether deciding about her own body or whether she will pursue a career at home or in the workplace, I will stand with her in celebrating that choice." Let's use our power to say, "I stand, arm-in-arm, with my sisters, regardless of who they are or the choices that they make, because I stand—unabashedly and unashamedly—for women's equality." Let's stand together and testify for each other, for our shared ideals, and when we do, we will be heard.

Wolf Whistle
Politics

Part I

Presidential Politics

The Woman Card

Jill Lepore

Jill Lepore is the David Woods Kemper '41 Professor of American History at Harvard University and a staff writer at the New Yorker, *where she has contributed since 2005. "The Woman Card" appeared in the* New Yorker *on June 27, 2016.*

"It means freedom for women to vote against the party this donkey represents" read the sign on a donkey named Woodrow who, wearing a bow, was paraded through Denver by the National Woman's Party during its campaign against the Democratic incumbent, President Wilson, in 1916. This year, the hundredth anniversary of the Woman's Party arrived, unnoticed, on June 5. Two days later, Hillary Clinton became the first woman to claim the presidential nomination of a major party: the Democratic Party.

If elected, Clinton will become the first female president in the nation's history. She will also join John Quincy Adams, James Monroe, Martin Van Buren, and James Buchanan as the only presidents to have served as both a senator and as secretary of state. If she loses the election to Donald Trump, he will be the first man elected president who has never served the public either in government or in the military. Trump wants to make America great again; Clinton wants to make history. That history is less about the last glass ceiling than about a party realignment as important as the Nixon-era Southern strategy, if less well known. Call it the Female Strategy.

For the past century, the edges of the parties have been defined by a debate about the political role and constitutional rights of women.

This debate is usually reduced to cant, as if the battle between the parties were a battle between the sexes. Republicans and Democrats are "just like men and women," Trent Lott liked to say: Democrats might be from Venus, but the GOP is "the party of Mars." Democrats have talked about a Republican "war on women"; Trump says, of Clinton, "The only card she has is the woman card." She polls better among women; he polls better among men. The immediacy and starkness of the contrast between the candidates obscures the historical realignment hinted at in their own biographies: she used to be a Republican and he used to be a Democrat. This election isn't a battle between the sexes. It is a battle between the parties, each hoping to win the votes of women without losing the votes of men. It's also marked by the sweeping changes to American politics caused by women's entry into public life. Long before women could vote, they carried into the parties a political style they had perfected first as abolitionists and then as prohibitionists: the moral crusade. No election has been the same since.

For a very long time, the parties had no idea what to do with women. At the nation's founding, women made an argument for female citizenship based on their role as mothers: in a republic, the civic duty of women is to raise sons who will be virtuous citizens. Federalists doffed their top hats, and no more. In the 1820s and '30s, Jacksonian democracy involved a lot of brawls: women were not allowed. When the social reformer Fanny Wright spoke at a political meeting in 1836, she was called a "female man." So instead, women entered public affairs by way of an evangelical religious revival that emphasized their moral superiority, becoming temperance reformers and abolitionists— and they wrote petitions. "The right of petitioning is the only political right that women have," Angelina Grimké pointed out in 1837.

The Whig Party was the first to make use of women in public, if ridiculously: in 1840, Tennessee women marched wearing sashes that read "Whig Husbands or None." Because neither the Whig Party nor the Democratic Party was able to address the question of slavery, a crop of new parties sprang up. Fueled by antislavery arguments, and adopting the style of moral suasion favored by female reformers, these parties tended to be welcoming to women, and even to arguments for women's rights.

The Republican Party was born in 1854, in Ripon, Wisconsin, when fifty-four citizens founded a party to oppose the Kansas-Nebraska Act, which threatened to create two new slave states. Three of those citizens were women. Women wrote Republican campaign literature and made speeches on behalf of the party. Its first presidential nominee, in 1856, was John Frémont, but more than one Republican observed that his wife, Jessie Benton Frémont, "would have been the better candidate." One of the Party's most popular and best-paid speakers was Anna Dickinson, who became the first woman to speak in the Hall of the House of Representatives.

The women's rights movement was founded in 1848. "It started right here in New York, a place called Seneca Falls," Clinton said in her victory speech on June 7, after effectively clinching the Democratic nomination. Advocates of women's rights were closely aligned with the Republican Party, and typically fought to end slavery and to earn for both black men and all women political equality with white men. In 1859, Elizabeth Cady Stanton wrote to Susan B. Anthony, "When I pass the gate of the celestials and good Peter asks me where I wish to sit, I will say, 'Anywhere so that I am neither a negro nor a woman. Confer on me, great angel, the glory of White manhood, so that henceforth I may feel unlimited freedom.'"

After Lincoln signed the Emancipation Proclamation, Stanton and Anthony gathered four hundred thousand signatures on petitions demanding the Thirteenth Amendment. They then began fighting for the Fourteenth Amendment, which they expected to guarantee the rights and privileges of citizenship for all Americans. Instead, they were told that "this is the Negro's hour," and that the amendment would include the word "male," so as to specifically exclude women. "Do you believe the African race is composed entirely of males?" Stanton asked Wendell Phillips. And then she warned, "If that word 'male' be inserted, it will take us a century at least to get it out."

The insertion of the word "male" into the Fourteenth Amendment had consequences that have lasted well into this year's presidential election. At the time, not everyone bought the argument that it was necessary to disenfranchise women in order to secure ratification. "Can any one tell us why the great advocates of Human Equality . . . forget that when they were a weak party and needed all the womanly strength of the nation to help them on, they always united the words 'without regard to sex, race, or color'?" one frustrated female supporter of the Republican Party asked. She could have found an answer in an observation made by Charles Sumner: "We know how the Negro will vote, but are not so sure of the women."

This election, many female voters, especially younger ones, resent being told that they should support Hillary Clinton just because she's a woman. It turns out that women don't form a political constituency any more than men do; like men, women tend to vote with their families and their communities. But in 1865 how women would vote was impossible to know. Would black women vote the way black men voted? Would white women vote like black women? The parties, led by white men, decided they'd just as soon not find out.

Women tried to gain the right to vote by simply seizing it, a plan that was known as the New Departure. Beginning in 1868, black and white women went to the polls all over the country and got arrested. Sojourner Truth tried to vote in Battle Creek, Michigan. In 1871, five black women were arrested for voting in South Carolina, months before Victoria Woodhull became the first woman to run for president. She announced that women already had the right to vote, under the privileges-and-immunities clause of the Constitution, and in 1871, she made this argument before the House Judiciary Committee. Anthony was arrested for voting in 1872—not for Woodhull but for the straight Republican ticket—and, in the end, the Supreme Court ruled against Woodhull's interpretation of the Constitution. Thus ended the New Departure.

Prevented from entering the electorate, women who wanted to influence public affairs were left to plead with men. For decades, these women had very little choice: whatever fight they fought, they had only the weapons of the nineteenth-century religious revival: the sermon, the appeal, the conversion, the crusade. The full measure of the influence of the female campaign on the American political style has yet to be taken. But that influence was felt first, and longest, in the Republican Party.

At the Republican nominating convention in 1872, the party split into two, but neither faction added a suffrage plank to its platform. "We recognize the equality of all men before the law," the Liberal Republicans declared, specifically discounting women. Stanton called the position taken by the regular Republicans—"the honest demand of any class of citizens for additional rights should be treated with respectful consideration"—not a plank but a splinter. Still, a splinter was more than suffragists ever got from the Democratic Party. In 1880, Anthony wrote a speech to deliver at the Democratic National Convention. It began: "To secure to twenty millions of women the rights of citizenship is to base your party on the eternal principles of justice." Instead, her statement was read by a male clerk while Anthony looked on, furious, after which, as the *Times* reported, "No action whatever was taken in regard to it, and Miss Anthony vexed the Convention no more."

Close elections seemed to be good for the cause because, in a tight race, both parties courted suffragists' support, but women soon discovered that this was fruitless: if they allied with Republicans, Democrats campaigned against Republicans by campaigning against suffrage. This led to a certain fondness for third parties—the Equal Rights Party, the Prohibition Party, the Home Protection Party. J. Ellen Foster, an Iowa lawyer who had helped establish the Woman's Christian Temperance Union, spoke at a Republican rally and cautioned that a third party rewards women's support with nothing more than flattery: "It gives to women seats in conventions and places their names on meaningless committees and tickets impossible of success." In 1892, Foster founded the Women's National Republican Association, telling the delegates at the party's convention that year, "We are here to help you. And we have come to stay."

In the second decade of the twentieth century, anticipating the ratification of the Nineteenth Amendment, the parties scrambled to secure the loyalty of voters who would double the size of the electorate, no less concerned than Sumner had been about how women would vote. "With a suddenness and force that have left observers gasping, women have injected themselves into the national campaign this year in a manner never before dreamed of in American politics," the *New York Herald* reported in 1912. When Theodore Roosevelt founded the Progressive Party, it adopted a suffrage plank, and he aggressively courted women. He considered appointing Jane Addams to his cabinet. At the Progressive Party's convention, Addams gave the second nominating speech. Then she grabbed a "Votes for Women" flag and marched it across the platform and up and down the auditorium. Roosevelt had tried to win the Republican nomination by bribing black delegates, who were then shut out of the Progressive Party's convention. When Addams got back to Chicago, she found a telegram from a black newspaper editor: "Woman suffrage will be stained with Negro Blood unless women refuse all alliance with Roosevelt."

Alice Paul, a feminist with a PhD from the University of Pennsylvania, who'd been arrested for fighting for suffrage in England, decided that American women ought to form their own party. "The name Woman's Party is open to a quite natural misunderstanding," Charlotte Perkins Gilman admitted, introducing the National Woman's Party in 1916. It wasn't a party, per se; it was a group of women whose strategy was to protest the existing parties, on the theory that no party could be trusted to advance the interests of women.

Terrified by the very idea of a party of women, the DNC formed a "Women's Division" in 1917, the RNC in 1918. The GOP pursued a policy of "complete amalgamation," its chairman pledging "to check any tendency toward the formation of a separate women's party." White women worked for both parties; black women worked only for the GOP, to fight the Democratic Party, which had become the party of southern whites. "The race is doomed unless Negro Women take an active part in local, state and national politics," the National League of Republican Colored Women said.

After 1920, Carrie Chapman Catt, the longtime head of the National American Woman Suffrage Association, turned her association into the League of Women Voters, providing voter education and other aids to good government. Meanwhile, she told women to join the parties: "The only way to get things in this country is to find them on the inside of the political party." Inside those parties, women fought for equal representation. In 1920, the Women's Division of the DNC implemented a rule mandating an equal number of male and female delegates. In 1923, the Republican National Committee introduced rule changes—billed as "seats for women"—that added bonus delegates for states that had voted Republican in the previous election. But the Democrats' fifty-fifty rule was observed only in the breach, and, as both Catherine E. Rymph and Melanie Gustafson have pointed out in their rich histories of women in the Republican Party, the real purpose of adding the new GOP seats was to reduce the influence of black southern delegates.

The League of Women Voters was nonpartisan, but the National Woman's Party remained antipartisan. It focused on securing passage of an Equal Rights Amendment, drafted by Paul, who had lately earned a law degree, and first introduced into Congress in 1923. Yet for all the work of the Woman's Party, the GOP was the party of women—or, rather, of white women—for most of the twentieth century. In the late 1920s and '30s, black men and women left the Republican Party, along with smaller numbers of white women, eventually forming a New Deal coalition of liberals, minorities, labor unionists, and, from the South, poor whites. FDR appointed Molly Williams Dewson the director of the DNC's Women's Division, which grew to eighty thousand members.

In 1937, determined to counter the efforts of the lady known as "More Women" Dewson, the RNC appointed Marion Martin its assistant chairman; during her tenure, she founded a national federation of women's clubs whose membership grew to four hundred thousand. Martin, thirty-seven and unmarried, had a degree in economics and had served a combined four terms in the Maine legislature. She led a moral crusade against the New Deal. In 1940, she also got the RNC to pass its own fifty-fifty rule and to endorse the Equal Rights Amendment, formally, in its platform. This went only so far. In 1946, Martin argued that party women needed more power. "We need it not because we are feminists," she said, "but because there are a great many non-partisan women's organizations that do wield an influence in this country." Five days later, she was forced to resign.

Hillary Rodham was born in Chicago in 1947. In 1960, when Richard Nixon ran against JFK, she checked voter lists for the GOP. By then, the majority of Republican Party workers were female. During the Cold War, the GOP boasted about "the women who work on the home front, ringing the doorbells, filling out registration cards, and generally doing the housework of government." As the historian Paula Baker has pointed out, party work is just like other forms of labor; women work harder, are paid less, are rarely promoted, and tend to enter a field when men begin to view it as demeaning. The elephant was the right symbol for the party, one senator said, because it has "a vacuum cleaner in front and a rug beater behind."

Betty Farrington, one of Martin's successors, turned the women's federation into a powerhouse of zealous crusaders. After Truman defeated Dewey in 1948, Farrington wanted the GOP to find its strongman:

> How thankful we would have been if a leader had appeared to show us the path to the promised land of our hope. The world needs such a man today. He is certain to come sooner or later. But we cannot sit idly by in the hope of his coming. Besides, his advent depends partly on us. The mere fact that a leader is needed does not guarantee his appearance. People must be ready for him, and we, as Republican women, in our clubs, prepare for him.

That man, many Republican voters today appear to believe, is Donald J. Trump, born in New York in 1946.

Political parties marry interests to constituencies. They are not defined by whether they attract women, particularly. Nor are they defined by their positions on equal rights for women and men. But no plausible history of American politics can ignore, first, the influence of a political style perfected, over a century, by citizens who, denied the franchise, were forced to plead, and, second, the effects of the doubling of the size of the electorate.

The Republican Party that is expected to nominate Trump was built by housewives and transformed by their political style, which men then made their own. The moral crusade can be found among nineteenth-century Democrats—William Jennings Bryan, say—but in the twentieth century it became the hallmark of the conservative wing of the Republican Party; it is the style, for instance, of Ted Cruz. This began in 1950, when the Republican Women's Club of Ohio County, West Virginia, invited Senator Joseph McCarthy as its principal speaker for Lincoln Day. It was during this speech that McCarthy said he had a list of subversives working at the State Department. "The great difference between our Western Christian world and the atheistic Communist world is not political—it is moral," McCarthy said. His rhetoric was that of the nineteenth-century women's crusade. The great crusader Barry Goldwater said in 1955, "If it were not for the National Federation of Republican Women, there would not be a Republican Party." That year, Republican women established Kitchen Cabinets, appointing a female equivalent to every member of Eisenhower's cabinet; their job was to share "political recipes on GOP accomplishments with the housewives of the nation," by sending monthly bulletins on "What's Cooking in Washington." One member of the Kitchen Cabinet was Phyllis Schlafly.

In 1963, Schlafly nominated Goldwater to speak at a celebration marking the twenty-fifth anniversary of the National Federation of Republican Women. In a straw poll taken after Goldwater delivered his speech, 262 out of 293 Federation delegates chose him. Meanwhile, Margaret Chase Smith was drafted into the race, a liberal alternative. As the historian Ellen Fitzpatrick recounts in her terrific new book *The Highest Glass Ceiling*, Smith was the first woman elected on her own to the Senate and the first woman to serve in both houses of Congress. Asked why she agreed to run against Goldwater, she once said, "There was nowhere to go but the Presidency." She was the first and boldest member of the Senate to oppose McCarthy, in a speech she made from the floor, known as the Declaration of Conscience: "I don't want to see the Republican Party ride to political victory on the Four Horsemen of Calumny—Fear, Ignorance, Bigotry, and Smear." At the convention in 1964, she refused to endorse Goldwater, and denied him her delegates.

Young Trump had little interest in politics. He liked the movies. In 1964, he graduated from military school, where he'd been known as a ladies' man, and thought about going to the University of Southern California, to study film. Hillary Rodham was a "Goldwater Girl." But Smith was her hero. She decided to run for president of her high school class, against a field of boys, and lost, "which did not surprise me," she wrote in her memoir, "but still hurt, especially because one of my opponents told me I was 'really stupid if I thought a girl could be elected president.'"

It's right about here that the GOP began to lose Hillary Rodham. In 1965, as a freshman at Wellesley, she was president of the Young

Republicans; she brought with her to college Goldwater's *The Conscience of a Conservative*. But Goldwater's defeat led to a struggle for the future of the party, and that struggle turned on Schlafly. In 1966, Elly Peterson, a Michigan state party chairman and supporter of George Romney, tried to keep Schlafly from becoming the president of the National Federation. "The nut fringe is beautifully organized," Peterson complained. At a three-thousand-woman Federation convention in 1967, Schlafly was narrowly defeated. Three months later, she launched her monthly newsletter. Rejecting the nascent women's liberation movement, she nevertheless blamed sexism for the GOP's failure to fully embrace its most strenuous conservatives:

> The Republican Party is carried on the shoulders of the women who do the work in the precincts, ringing doorbells, distributing literature, and doing all the tiresome, repetitious campaign tasks. Many men in the Party frankly want to keep the women doing the menial work, while the selection of candidates and the policy decisions are taken care of by the men in the smoke-filled rooms.

In the summer of 1968, Trump graduated from Wharton, where, he later said, he spent most of his time reading the listings of foreclosures on federally financed housing projects. That September, in Atlantic City, feminists staged a protest at the Miss America pageant, the sort of pageant that Trump would one day buy, run, and cherish. They carried signs reading "Welcome to the Cattle Auction."

Rodham, a twenty-year-old Capitol Hill intern, attended the Republican National Convention in Miami as a supporter of the antiwar candidate, Nelson Rockefeller. For the first time since 1940, the GOP dropped from its platform its endorsement of equal rights. Rodham went home to see her family, and, hiding the fact from her parents, drove downtown to watch the riots outside the Democratic National Convention. One month too young to vote, she'd supported the antiwar Democrat, Eugene McCarthy, before the convention, but later said she would probably have voted for the party's nominee, Hubert Humphrey.

In 1969, Rodham, senior class president at Wellesley, became the first student invited to deliver a commencement address, a speech that was featured in *Life*. In 1970, a leader of her generation, a student at Yale Law School, and wearing a black armband mourning the students killed at Kent State, she spoke about her opposition to the Vietnam War at a convention of the League of Women Voters on the occasion of its fiftieth anniversary. She had become a feminist, and a Democrat.

What followed is more familiar. Between 1964 and 1980, Schlafly's arm of the party steadily gained control of the GOP, which began courting evangelical Christians, including white male Southern Democrats alienated by their party's civil rights agenda. In the wake of *Roe v. Wade*, and especially after the end of the Cold War, the Republican Party's new crusaders turned their attention from communism to abortion. The Democratic Party became the party of women, partly by default. For a long time, it could have gone another way.

In 1971, Hillary Rodham met Bill Clinton, Donald Trump took over the family business, and Gloria Steinem, Tanya Melich, Bella Abzug, and Shirley Chisholm helped found the National Women's Political Caucus, which, like the National Woman's Party, sought to force both parties to better represent women and to gain passage of the Equal Rights Amendment. At the 1972 Republican National Convention in Miami, Republican feminists demanded that the party restore its ERA plan to the platform. They won, but at a cost. After the convention, Schlafly founded STOP ERA.

The Democratic Party, meanwhile, was forging a new coalition. "A new hat, or rather a bonnet, was tossed into the Democratic presidential race today," Walter Cronkite said on CBS News, when Chisholm, the first black woman to be elected to Congress, announced her bid. She went all the way to the convention. Chisholm said, "You can go to that Convention and you can yell, 'Woman power! Here I come!' You can yell, 'Black power! Here I come!' The only thing those hard-nosed boys are going to understand at that Convention: 'How many delegates you got?'" She got a hundred and fifty-two.

By 1973, Trump was making donations to the Democratic Party. "The simple fact is that contributing money to politicians is very standard and accepted for a New York City developer," he explains in *The Art of the Deal*. He also appeared, for the first time, in a story in the *New York Times*, with the headline "Major Landlord Accused of Antiblack

Bias in City." The Department of Justice had charged Trump and his father with violating the 1968 Fair Housing Act. "We never have discriminated," Trump told the *Times*, "and we never would."

In 1974, Rodham moved to Washington, DC, where she worked for the special counsel preparing for the possible impeachment of Richard Nixon. The next year, she married Bill Clinton, though she didn't take his name. The GOP, weakened by Watergate, and thinking to stanch the flow of departing women, elected as party chair Mary Louise Smith, an ardent feminist. In 1975, some thirty GOP feminists formed the Republican Women's Task Force to support the ERA, reproductive rights, affirmative action, federally funded childcare, and the extension of the Equal Pay Act.

The shift came in 1976. Rodham went to the Democratic National Convention, at Madison Square Garden. Schlafly went to the Republican Convention, in Kansas City, where, as the political scientist Jo Freeman has argued, feminists won the battle but lost the war. For the nomination, Ford, a supporter of the ERA, defeated Reagan, an opponent, but the platform committee defeated the ERA by a single vote.

In 1980, Republican feminists knew they'd lost when Reagan won the nomination; even so moderate a Republican as George Romney called supporters of the ERA "moral perverts," and the platform committee urged a constitutional ban on abortion. Tanya Melich, a Republican feminist, began talking about a "Republican War Against Women," a charge Democrats happily made their own. Mary Crisp, a longtime RNC co-chair, was forced out, and declared of the party of Lincoln and of Anthony, "We are reversing our position and are about to bury the rights of over a hundred million American women under a heap of platitudes."

Buried they remain. Until 1980, during any presidential election for which reliable data exist and in which there had been a gender gap, the gap had run one way: more women than men voted for the Republican candidate. That changed when Reagan became the GOP nominee; more women than men supported Carter, by eight percentage points. Since then, the gender gap has never favored a GOP presidential candidate. The Democratic Party began billing itself as the party of women. By 1987, Trump had become a Republican.

In the Reagan era, Republican strategists believed that, in trading women for men, they'd got the better end of the deal. As the Republican consultant Susan Bryant pointed out, Democrats "do so badly among men that the fact that we don't do quite as well among women becomes irrelevant." And that's more or less where it lies.

With the end of the ERA, whose chance at ratification expired in 1982, both parties abandoned a political settlement necessary to the stability of the republic. The entrance of women into politics on terms that are, fundamentally and constitutionally, unequal to men's has produced a politics of interminable division, infused with misplaced and dreadful moralism. Republicans can't win women; when they win, they win without them, by winning with men. Democrats need to win both the black vote and the female vote. Trump and Clinton aren't likely to break that pattern. Trump, with his tent-revival meetings, is crusading not only against Clinton and against Obama but against immigrants, against Muslims, and, in the end, against every group of voters that has fled the Republican Party, as he rides with his Four Horsemen: Fear, Ignorance, Bigotry, and Smear.

"This is a movement of the American people," Trump wrote in an e-mail to supporters. "And the American people never lose." It took a very long time, and required the work of the Republican Party, to change the meaning of "the American people" to include everyone. It hasn't taken very long at all for Trump to change it back. The next move is Clinton's, and her party's.

The Woman's Party

Namara Smith

Namara Smith is a contributing editor at N+1 *and writes for the* New Yorker, Literary Hub, *and more. "The Woman's Party" appeared in* N+1 *in fall 2016.*

One of the more telling exchanges of the Democratic elections took place this past February, when Rachel Maddow, moderating the New Hampshire primary debate, asked Hillary Clinton to respond to Bernie Sanders's charge that she was not a true progressive. Clinton answered that she was "a progressive who likes to get things done"—and accused Sanders of sitting out the past three decades of Democratic politics. "Every step along the way I have stood up and fought," she said, "and have the scars to prove it."

Sanders noted that Clinton had previously called herself a moderate, and that it was impossible to be both a moderate and a progressive. "Secretary Clinton," he said, "does represent the establishment. I represent, I hope, ordinary Americans."

Clinton answered: "Senator Sanders is the only person who would characterize me, a woman running to be the first woman president, as exemplifying the establishment. . . . It is really quite amusing to me. People support me because they know me. They know my life's work."

The moment captured the gulf between the candidates. Both seemed utterly confident of the truth of what they were saying; both seemed utterly scornful of the other's claims. Behind Clinton's assertion was the certainty of a woman who has embodied the social transformations of the sixties for millions of people since being photographed for *Life*'s feature on the 1969 student protests, and has spent the past thirty years being attacked by the right as a radical feminist. Behind Sanders's words was the stubbornness of a man who openly declared himself a socialist at the height of the Cold War and has spent the past thirty years being ignored for the sake of his principles. Bernie is as much a militant socialist as Hillary is a radical feminist—that is, not very—but both represent the furthest encroachments of these traditions on American liberalism. For Clinton, this is second-wave feminism and the social movements of the sixties. For Sanders, it is the social democracy of the midcentury New Deal and Great Society.

These traditions—feminism and social protection—have a common history, and their most visible point of intersection and conflict is welfare. Debates over welfare cut to the quick of divergent feminist politics in America, between "equality" and "difference" feminists, and welfare, more than anything else, is the issue defining Clinton's primary campaign. Even before she championed the welfare-reform bill her husband signed in 1996, Clinton took a side in the debate simply by being who she was and pursuing the path she did. Her shortcomings as a feminist candidate trace back to this debate, which has yet to be resolved.

The feminist conflict over welfare began in the 1910s, when the women's suffrage movement brought feminists and progressive social reformers together. The most radical group in the coalition, Alice Paul's National Woman's Party, proved instrumental in gaining public support for the Nineteenth Amendment, but when Paul pushed for a new constitutional measure that would guarantee women's rights in all fields, proposing the Equal Rights Amendment in 1923, her allies from the suffrage movement came out strongly against the bill.

Women from the National Consumers' League and the National Women's Trade Union League—adherents to the progressive tradition of social reform—identified strongly with the maternal values of selfless care and devotion to the welfare of others, which went against the ERA's presumption of equality between men and women. These "maternalists," as they came to be known, fought for state laws that restricted working hours for women and children, protected them from unsafe labor conditions, and provided small pensions to widows and single mothers. While Paul and the Woman's Party claimed such leg-islation set a dangerous legal precedent, the maternalists countered that the proposed amendment failed to take into account the situation of working-class women—a uniquely vulnerable group with dual ob-ligations to family and wage earning that forced them into working a "double day." Rather than asserting women's equality with men, they argued for recognition of their differences. "The inescapable facts," wrote Florence Kelley in *The Nation* in 1922, are "that men do not bear children, are freed from the burdens of maternity, and are not susceptible, in the same measure as women, to poisons now increas-ingly characteristic of certain industries, and to the universal poison of fatigue." What most women needed, they argued, was not a blanket guarantee of political and legal equality with men but the economic security provided by protective legislation.

Both sides enlisted support from male allies. The Woman's Party made common cause with business interests that benefited from un-regulated access to women's cheap labor, and the maternalists were backed by trade unionists who saw protective labor regulations as a way to keep women from competing for men's jobs. As the labor move-ment gained influence in the 1930s, the maternalists' power grew, and they succeeded in blocking the passage of the ERA indefinitely. When FDR was elected in 1933, many prominent maternalists were appointed to his administration, including his secretary of labor, Fran-ces Perkins, which enabled them to play a decisive role in shaping the federal welfare state.

But while the maternalists' protective legislation laid the ground-work for the New Deal's federal labor regulations, the specifics were left to the men. Many of the benefits enshrined in the New Deal were tied to employment, but the drafters were careful to distinguish among different types of work, providing generous benefits to some work-ers and none to others. The Fair Labor Standards Act, which set the first federal minimum-wage and maximum-hours laws; the National Labor Relations Act, which guaranteed workers the right to bargain collectively; and Social Security's old-age and unemployment insur-ance programs did not extend to many low-paid workers, including farm laborers, maids, housekeepers, laundresses, child-care workers, and companions to the elderly, thus excluding most women, as well as black men, from the economic security and political recognition these laws afforded to the white male industrial working class.

Meanwhile, the maternalists' efforts focused on a supplemental form of public assistance called Aid to Dependent Children—the origins of what came to be called, simply, welfare. Designed as a federal grant that would add to the money states spent on their own public-assistance programs, ADC was meant to augment the state pensions for single mothers that had been a central victory of maternalist policy in the 1910s. By leaving these pensions intact, ADC inherited many of their flaws. The programs, which relied on an understanding of widows and children as innocent victims of misfortune, had stringent eligibility requirements. Recipients had to prove that they were both legitimately in need and "morally fit." Their beneficiaries, many of whom were immigrant mothers, had to go through a lengthy verification process to prove that their incomes were too low to support them, and were instructed to take English classes, to attend church, to stop cooking with garlic. Benefits were set deliberately low to discourage single motherhood.

The Woman's Party had warned in 1923 that protective legislation could be used to keep women confined to "the lowest, worst paid labor." Their fears turned out to be well founded. In the 1940s and '50s, the surest way for white women to enter the postwar middle class was not through work, but through marriage; black women, because black men were also excluded from the benefits of downward redistribution, were denied even this option. Well into the 1960s, newspapers divided help-wanted ads into men's and women's sections, reflecting the material differences in opportunity, security, and income that separated one class of worker from the other. The labor market was more segregated by sex than it had been half a century earlier: three-quarters of women in the workforce worked in female-dominated fields, largely in the service industry, with limited job security or possibility of advancement. Single women's jobs were designed on the assumption that at any moment they might get married and quit; married women's jobs were designed on the assumption that at any moment they might get pregnant and quit. Pregnant women who showed signs of not wanting to quit their jobs were often dismissed with no unemployment benefits. A man with a high school degree earned more, on average, than a woman with a bachelor's degree.

When the second-wave feminist movement broke out in the 1960s, it was with the returned force of decades of denial and repression. The ideas that seemed radical when Alice Paul called for them in 1923—that women deserved to be treated as individuals, rather than as wives and mothers, and to compete on equal terms with men in all areas of life—were suddenly embraced by hundreds of thousands of suburban housewives. Much of the movement's political energy was devoted to breaking down the formal obstacles to women's participation in the primary labor force, and some of its most significant victories involved overturning the protective legislation the maternalists had erected.

More than forty years later, Hillary Clinton is perhaps the most visible beneficiary of this social transformation. She is by an order of magnitude the most powerful woman in American politics, and unlike her hero Eleanor Roosevelt, she was not born into a political dynasty. Instead, like our two most recent Democratic presidents, she is a product of the postwar American university system. Her success is a testament to the gulf between the old order and the new opportunities that were available to women who were positioned to take advantage of them. In 1969 she was one of twenty-seven women admitted to Yale Law School out of a class of more than two hundred, in 1978 the first female chair of the Legal Services Corporation, in 2001 the first female senator from New York—and now the first female presidential nominee of a major US political party, a milestone that would have been difficult to imagine in 1947, the year she was born.

Clinton's origin story is by now one of the representative histories of the baby boomers, the second-wave equivalent of a log-cabin narrative. She was born in Chicago and grew up in the postwar suburbs, the daughter of a dependent housewife with a high school degree and of a domestic tyrant who beat his children and kept tight control of the family purse strings. When Hillary first left for Wellesley College, she was a Republican. When she graduated, in 1969, she was a member of the New Left who had been involved in the campus antiwar movement, marched for civil rights, written her senior thesis on Saul Alinsky, pressured her college to remove in loco parentis regulations, and given the school's first student commencement address, in which she called for "more immediate, ecstatic, and penetrating modes of living." After college, she moved to Berkeley, California, and interned at Robert Treuhaft's radical law firm, campaigned for George McGovern, and became involved in the left-wing movement for children's rights, advocating that children be recognized as autonomous legal entities rather than dependents of their parents.

For three decades, Clinton has been a public face of second-wave feminism. She has been a focal point of conservative attacks since Pat Buchanan made her the centerpiece of his famous culture-wars speech at the 1992 Republican National Convention. ("What does Hillary believe? Well, Hillary believes that twelve-year-olds should have the right to sue their parents. And Hillary has compared marriage and the family, as institutions, to slavery and life on an Indian reservation. . . . This, my friends—this is radical feminism.") You could assemble a montage of public anxieties over the figure of the career woman of the eighties and nineties using nothing but moments from her life: her vacillation over whether to take her husband's last name, her decision to wait until her thirties to have a child, her pantsuits, her hair. "I suppose I could have stayed home and baked cookies." "I'm not some little woman standing by my man."

As she moved to the mainstream of national politics, Clinton modulated her earlier opinions, but she has continually insisted on women's liberation from traditional forms of authority through participation in the paid workforce. The embrace of the market as a tool for women's emancipation is the basis of her alliance with the New Democrats and her reputation as a champion of female entrepreneurship. It is this vision that lies behind her support for her husband's campaign promise to "end welfare as we know it" in 1991.

Bill introduced his plan to dismantle welfare, by that point called Aid to Families with Dependent Children, or AFDC, early in his campaign. Speaking before students at Georgetown in fall 1991, he claimed that the "New Covenant" he wanted to offer the American people could "break the cycle of welfare":

> Welfare should be a second chance, not a way of life. In my administration we're going to put an end to welfare as we have come to know it. I want to erase the stigma of welfare for good

by restoring a simple, dignified principle: no one who can work can stay on welfare forever. We'll still help people to help themselves. And those who need education and training and child care and medical coverage for their kids—they'll get it. We'll give them all the help they need and we'll keep them on public assistance for up to two years, but after that, people who are able to work, they'll have to go to work, either in the private sector or through a community service job. No more permanent dependence on welfare as a way of life.

At the time, AFDC was perhaps the most widely reviled program in government history. Since its passage in 1935, it had become a symbol of everything that was wrong with redistributive government programs. Among its most vociferous critics were welfare recipients themselves, who were subjected to a battery of moral tests and denied the dignity and title of a worker, no matter how much unwaged housework and childcare they did. Although AFDC gave all unemployed mothers the right to benefits, states were free to set additional eligibility limits, and many did. In 1943, Louisiana became the first state to institute "employable mother" laws, popular in the rural South, which suspended benefits to mothers at planting and harvesttime. "Suitable home," "man in the house," and "substitute father" laws denied benefits to mothers who caseworkers could prove were having regular sex, the regulations being loose enough that "regular" was interpreted as anywhere from once a week to once every six months. Social workers were often sent to examine the homes of welfare recipients, searching for unwashed dishes and unmade beds. How you were treated depended on where you lived: the laws tended to be harsher in regions with more black mothers on welfare. Payments in the South were, on average, about half as large as in other parts of the country. As black Americans migrated to the North's industrial cities, those cities' welfare laws became more restrictive.

In 1967, civil rights activists and welfare mothers formed the National Welfare Rights Organization to reframe as an entitlement what had long been seen as a form of public charity. Activists argued that unpaid domestic labor should be recognized as a form of work and granted the dignity allocated to work. Welfare, they insisted, was a right, not a handout. Rather than a stigmatized, bureaucratically administered payment, the NWRO called for a universal Guaranteed Adequate Income for poor men, women, and children regardless of marital or employment status.

The welfare movement's leaders saw welfare as something that concerned all women. "Welfare's like a traffic accident," wrote Johnnie Tillmon, one of the founders of the NWRO, in her classic essay "Welfare Is a Women's Issue." "It can happen to anybody, but especially it happens to women." Mothers, as the maternalists had recognized, had less bargaining power than other workers; they lacked the freedom of motion and flexibility of single men. From this perspective, welfare was unemployment insurance for the most vulnerable members of the workforce. It gave women the power to hold out for better jobs and to leave abusive relationships. But the broader feminist movement failed to incorporate this insight. Although prominent feminists such as Shirley Chisholm, Bella Abzug, Gloria Steinem, and then president of NOW Aileen Hernandez vocally supported welfare rights, the movement's central focus remained formal equality in the workplace. As women in government and organized labor who had previously favored maternalist policies began to throw their weight behind the struggle for equal rights, welfare became a punching bag for conservative politicians advocating increasingly punitive work requirements.

Having abandoned the maternalists' sentimental defense of motherhood as a sacred calling, most second-wave feminists had no terms in which to mount a convincing justification for income support to poor mothers. Other women were working; why shouldn't they work too? But for middle-class women, work meant public recognition, self-determination, the right to be seen as autonomous individuals and to participate in civic life. For welfare mothers, especially black women, who made up two-thirds of all domestic workers by 1960, it meant watching other women's children, preparing their food, and scrubbing their floors, services that professional women increasingly relied on as they entered the workforce in greater numbers. The version of welfare reform Bill Clinton envisioned was much more generous than the bill eventually passed by the Republican Congress in 1996. It would have included child-care and job-placement programs—but it would still have required welfare recipients to work. Hillary's support for the bill reveals the deep fault lines of class and race that fractured the second-wave feminist movement, as white middle-class women purchased their independence from domestic labor by shifting the burden to working-class women of color.

The welfare reform that was signed into law effectively ended all direct, cash-based public assistance. While earlier welfare programs included work requirements but tacitly protected recipients who were unable to find jobs, this one instituted strict time limits. The bill stipulated that states have less than 20 percent of welfare recipients on the rolls for more than five years, and that 50 percent of all single mothers on welfare be employed. "The bill closes its eyes to all the facts and complexities of the real world and essentially says to recipients, Find a job," wrote Peter Edelman, Clinton's former assistant secretary of the Department of Health and Human Services, in a widely circulated article called "The Worst Thing Bill Clinton Has Done." The money was allocated in the form of block grants, meaning that each state received a fixed amount of money and full control of how to distribute it, thus wiping out decades of hard-won federal legislative protections of AFDC. The result was to sharply reduce the number of people on welfare. Some states threw 90 percent of recipients off the rolls, a result many of the bill's advocates managed to celebrate as a sign of its success.

Twenty years later, the bill's catastrophic effects are obvious. The number of people in extreme poverty—those living on less than $2 a day—rose from 636,000 in 1996 to 1.65 million in 2011, prompting the *Financial Times* to compare the US unfavorably to Russia, Jordan, and the West Bank. Reverting to an entirely state-directed model has meant more racial discrimination. (Oregon, for instance, where 80 percent of welfare recipients are white, has some of the most generous welfare policies; Louisiana, where more than 80 percent are black, has some of the least.) And because Congress decided to save money by not indexing the block grants to inflation, their real value has already decreased by a third. Clinton expanded the Earned Income Tax Credit to offset some of these cuts, but the credit was tied to regular employment. As a result, although the working poor have been protected to a certain extent, there has been almost no cash assistance for those without steady work, a provision that has disproportionately hurt women, especially single mothers.

In her memoir *Living History*, published in 2003, when welfare reform was still broadly seen as a success, Hillary claimed credit for whipping Congress to vote for the Personal Responsibility and Work Opportunity Reconciliation Act. "This was a historic opportunity," she wrote of the bill, "to change a system oriented toward dependence to one that encouraged independence." Her support for welfare reform was couched in the rhetoric of women's empowerment through work ("work that gives structure, meaning, and dignity to most of our lives"). She framed the bill's work requirements in terms of the contest between "dependency" and "dignity," saying, "Too many of those on welfare had known nothing but dependency all their lives, and many would have found it difficult to make the transition to work on their own."

Women's economic empowerment was at the heart of Clinton's politics in the 1990s, and it has been at the heart of her message this year. But her call "to systematically and relentlessly pursue more economic opportunity" for women, as she put it in a speech at the Asia-Pacific Economic Cooperation forum several years ago, has failed to move younger women, who voted overwhelmingly against her in the Democratic primaries. The belief that what's best for the market is best for women, which has powered her political career for decades, has lost much of its force, and the promises of empowerment feminism have grown increasingly threadbare. Women now make up half the paid workforce but are still disproportionately represented in the lowest-paying and least-protected jobs. They consistently make less than men across all industries and are still clustered in female-dominated occupations. Mothers, in particular, face steep economic penalties. Having a child, according to a study by Elizabeth Warren and her daughter and reported in 2003, was the single best predictor that a woman would declare bankruptcy.

But if the political order that Clinton represents is showing signs of exhaustion, a new one has not emerged to take its place. During the Democratic primaries, Sanders campaigned against her by appealing to a pastoral vision of the midcentury welfare state that hid the exclusions and political compromises that led to its collapse. His campaign brought the word "class" back into national politics, but he sometimes seemed to speak to a phantom of the old white male industrial working class rather than to the black, brown, and female service workers who make up the majority of the working class today.

Nowhere are the limits of Sanders's picture of the welfare state clearer than in his stance on welfare itself. If welfare is Clinton's weakest point, the thread that, when tugged, begins to unravel her moral legitimacy and claim to represent women's interests, it was a weakness that Sanders was unable to exploit. Although he tried to attack Clinton's support for welfare reform, he was hampered by the fact that his own proposals did not provide much of an alternative. His campaign's official position on welfare was that "nobody who works forty hours a week should live in poverty," and his preferred models for public assistance, like Clinton's, were tied to full-time employment. Although Sanders's call for tuition-free public higher education and universal health care has helped to reframe both as universal entitlements rather than commodities, he has not made a similar case for welfare.

In one of her early essays, the political philosopher Nancy Fraser argues that all existing welfare states have foundered on the question of what role to allot women. As long as women perform a disproportionate share of reproductive labor, she claims, redistributive programs based solely on employment will privilege men, even if accompanied by full-employment programs and universal childcare. But the alternative— designating primary caregivers as a separate, sheltered class—is no better. Even if caregiver benefits were officially gender-neutral, their recipients would still be disproportionately female, which reinforces the sexual division of labor and leaves women underrepresented in public life. Both choices are bad; neither, as Fraser says, asks men to change.

Fraser's answer is to propose what she calls a "universal caregiver" model based on the assumption that all workers are also caregivers and all caregivers are also workers. Conceiving a new welfare state based on this model would mean rethinking the length of the workday, socializing childcare, decoupling Social Security and health insurance from employment, and returning to the welfare rights movement's call for a guaranteed minimum income. Above all, it would mean placing feminist insights and concerns at the center, rather than the periphery, of any left politics. If the movement that Sanders's campaign called into being is going to embody the spirit of a new revolution, this would be a good place to start.

Which Women Support Hillary (and Which Women Can't Afford To)

Sarah Leonard

Sarah Leonard is a senior editor at The Nation *and co-editor of* The Future We Want: Radical Ideas for a New Century. *She is a contributing editor to* Dissent *and the* New Inquiry. *"Which Women Support Hillary (and Which Women Can't Afford To)" appeared in* The Nation *on February 17, 2016.*

I'm going to posit something radical: the most vocal support for Hillary Clinton comes from women in the commentariat, very much like myself, who have had to fight sexism to succeed in public-facing, white-collar professions and relate to Hillary's struggle to do the same. Many of these women have also engaged in other struggles that are the opposite of Hillary's—women like Sady Doyle, Amanda Marcotte, and my own colleague Katha Pollitt are foes of Wall Street and imperial misadventure, while Hillary has often been a friend to the wealthy, and a hawk. A quote from Lena Dunham, stumping for Hillary in Iowa, captures the sentiment well: "As a newly grown-up woman who has experienced my fair share of backlash, public shaming and puritanical judgments, that [Hillary's resistance to sexist attacks] really moves me." And it's not just true for someone thrust into fame as quickly as Dunham. Every well-known feminist is subjected to the same language on Twitter that is directed toward Hillary Clinton on the campaign trail: bitch, harpy, dumb, ugly, and so on. As Doyle writes, "Her story moves me . . . simply as an example of a woman who got every misogynist trick in the world thrown at her, and who didn't let it slow her down. On that level, she's actually become a bit of a personal role model." To quote another Clinton, we feel her pain.

There is a part of our own pain that we hope Hillary Clinton will fix. Marcotte, no stranger to misogynist trolls of all stripes, writes that "yes, having a woman president does matter, if only to spend election night watching the spreading urine stains on the pants of the men who spent months lecturing feminists." Erica Brazelton wrote in these pages in June 2013 that "seeing said bodies in spaces not originally reserved for them matters." Or to quote Sady Doyle, "When people yell at me, or dislike me, I no longer think oh, how horrible this is for me. I now think, well, if Hillary can do it. Seriously. If Hillary Clinton can be called an evil hag by major media outlets for most of her adult life and run for president, I can deal with blocking ten or twenty guys on Twitter." Some of those guys are Sanders supporters; much digital ink has been spilled over the presence of "Bernie bros," or dudes whose support for their candidate is expressed by being assholes to Hillary supporters. In other words, Hillary Clinton's professional success represents one step closer to a meritocracy, where every little girl (and boy) knows that a woman can be president, and that this might trickle down to all of our workplaces, allowing each professional young woman to be taken a bit more seriously. To quote Kanye West's timeless words, her presence itself is a gift—what she does is of secondary importance.

This is a really interesting argument, because it is not, of course, very easy to measure the power of example. But let's try. Some countries have tried to create policy around female representation. For example, lawmakers in Norway noticed that women were vastly underrepresented on corporate boards. So, in 2003, they passed a requirement that 40 percent of every LLC board be female. Eleven years later, a study found "no evidence of significant differential improvements for women in the post-reform cohort, either in terms of average earnings or likelihood of filling in a top position in a Norwegian business." Women still, by and large, take time off to raise children and suffer from sexism in promotions. There has, however, been another Nordic model that's worked quite well. In 1995, Sweden put in place a policy that not only offered generous parental leave, but motivated both men and women to take it by offering some months of parental leave that would be lost if men didn't take advantage of them. This counteracted the effects of entrenched sexism (women would stay home and fall behind, while men did not). Today, things aren't perfect, but women take 75 percent of parental leave, as opposed to 99.5 percent in 1974, and Sweden has ranked in the top four countries for gender equality since the World Economic Forum introduced their gender gap rankings in 2006. In other words, bright examples are a pretty inefficient way to create change, while interventions in the workplace and the distribution of wealth works pretty well.

To take another example, Sheryl Sandberg, the author of *Lean In*, has become a model for white-collar women everywhere; I have been critical of her book, but in reading it found plenty of information that applies to my white-collar workplace that I could plausibly take as advice. Her example and encouragement are no doubt a great boon for women committed to working in competitive Silicon Valley start-ups. At the same time, Sandberg's example only goes so far—it doesn't do much good to tell a housekeeper to "lean in"—she'd just be doing more work for her boss, with no gain for her, buying into a system emotionally that exploits her physically. And in fact, when Sheryl Sandberg visited Harvard, in part to celebrate women in business, she was petitioned by housekeepers at a Harvard-owned hotel who hoped that she would "lean in" with them as part of their campaign for a union and better working conditions. She declined. They ultimately gained a union anyway and have seen work abuses drop and income increase.

All of this is to say something pretty self-evident if you think about it: example and representation is probably pretty important within a class. It's hard to prove, but our gut tells us that role models matter. The mere existence of female leaders can inspire confidence in others who have opportunities and just need that extra strength to seize them. What representation is pretty bad at doing is affecting who gets those opportunities—if you're poor, no positive example is gonna just boost you out of it. That's an old right-wing myth—if you can look up at your superiors, you can tug your bootstraps in their direction.

Others have cataloged Hillary Clinton's opposition to policies that would redistribute wealth and power toward women à la the Nordic model, so I'll keep that brief here. Suffice to say that she has spoken about women caring for their children on welfare with venom and has made herself an enemy of the poor. She is surely not the most egregious opponent of women's well-being—she is, after all, pro-choice—but her allies, practically speaking, are big donors like Goldman Sachs and Walmart, which lobby hard against redistribution and good treatment of women in the workplace. Voting for Hillary is, unfortunately, a strike against poor people.

So, to support Hillary Clinton is to support a genuinely good example for white-collar women's behavior when trying to beat sexism at work at the expense of policies that might help the majority of women. Or is that a false dichotomy?

Some believe that the presence of Bernie Sanders in the race has offered an alternative—his policies redistribute more, and he is a self-professed feminist, but . . . he is a man. No inspiring grit-in-the-face-of-sexism to be had in this old white dude. He is, however, a socialist and, if you haven't figured it out already, I think socialism is women's best hope because it accounts for the policies that will get them the stuff they need. His policies are better for more women because they're more redistributive.

"When we heard Bernie Sanders talking about everything we've been talking about it was a no brainer," says Karen Higgins, one of three co-presidents of the National Nurses Union and a nurse for the last forty years. She's spent the last thirty-seven working in intensive care and at sixty-two still works full-time at Boston Medical Center. When I spoke with her, she was home preparing to go campaign for Sanders in New Hampshire. The NNU has endorsed him, citing his longtime alignment on their trademark issues: single-payer health care, taxing Wall Street, less college debt for their kids, and opposition to the Trans-Pacific Partnership (TPP), which includes concessions to pharmaceutical companies. Contrary to much commentary on the left, the nurses don't regard a commitment to single payer as foolishly ideological: Higgins describes receiving intensive care patients whose first question is what the treatment will cost and how they can pay. She differentiates between an insurance system (Obamacare) and universal health care, which would eliminate the need for individuals to wrangle with private companies. It's been a long time since a serious candidate carried a commitment to this system as a banner issue. The nurses of the 90 percent female union, as a result, have found themselves more inspired by Sanders.

When I ask Higgins about gender, she does seem a tad regretful. "There's a piece of me as a woman that would definitely have loved to see a woman in that position, so there's a little bit of a heartbreak that she did not come out as strong" on the nurses' issues. "It would be nice if she had taken a stance." What does she think of the Twitter phenomenon of Bernie bros? "I don't think I've seen that one. I'm not good about Twitter."

The argument that a Clinton presidency would increase respect for women, while a Sanders presidency would do nothing to create greater gender equity is belied by the experience of nurses and the people they serve. Hillary might face sexism at work, and so might white-collar women, but so do the nurses—they do care work largely assigned to women that has enjoyed little support from the government in terms of funding, wages, and reasonable structures of care. The problems that afflict the majority of women can only be resolved in the realm of organizing, policymaking, and other large-scale efforts. The proper question for a presidential election is who will forward these big programs. It is absolutely possible to fight sexism at work, come home, and abuse the help. One could argue that Hillary has done this on a national scale. "I hate to say this to women," says Higgins, "but that has to be the real priority, whether it's a man or a woman—what it'll take to get people back on their feet in this country and take care of them."

Black Feminists Don't Owe Hillary Clinton Their Support

Kirsten West Savali

Kirsten West Savali is a cultural critic and an associate editor at The
Root. *"Black Feminists Don't Owe Hillary Clinton Their Support" ap-*
peared in The Root *on February 3, 2016.*

Over the course of the last few days, I have been accused of both
protecting and vilifying Democratic presidential candidate Hillary
Clinton. The reason for this is as simple as it is complex: people of
color, especially black women, have to hold so many things in ten-
sion regarding race, gender, and class that depending on whom they
find themselves in conversations with, it appears as if one facet is being prioritized over the other. This is why, when we're speaking about
Hillary Rodham Clinton and the major two-party political system, it's
imperative that we make it plain. Clinton's candidacy is evidence of
why intersectionality is so critical, because for black women existing
on those fault lines of race, gender, and class, not much improves for us
regardless of who is in the White House; nor does it matter for which
party we carry the banner.

This does not equate to support for the Republican Party, though
I've had that accusation hurled at me as well. Marco Rubio's voice is
like nails on a chalkboard; Ted Cruz is like some political science
experiment gone horribly, horribly wrong; Donald Trump's rallying
cry should be "Heil Trump!"; and Carly Fiorina, the lone woman in
the pack, is traipsing about making references to fabricated Planned

Parenthood videos that look as if a fourteen-year-old techie created them in iMovie. The racist and misogynist policies they propose are dangerously regressive and primarily serve wealthy white, Christian men holding on for dear life to maintain their supremacy.

Still, Clinton herself has said that she and Republicans get along just fine when she's in office. Both Clinton and Bernie Sanders—the largely beloved senator from Vermont and her Iowa co-front-runner—have been vocal about their nonsupport for reparations. Both of them have the same weak stance on Israel's illegal occupation of Palestine and our country's complicity in it. They also support drone warfare, just like President Barack Obama and President George W. Bush before them.

The 1994 Violent Crime Control and Law Enforcement Act—which Hillary Clinton lobbied for, Sanders voted for, Vice President Joe Biden authored, and President Bill Clinton signed—shows why black women shouldn't just follow the Democratic Party by default, even if the front-runner is a woman. Mass incarceration and its tentacles have been disastrous for black America. On everything from HIV and AIDS to poverty, crime, limited access to a quality education, destruction of families, and recidivism most often due to difficulties finding and maintaining employment, the law has been disastrous. Then, in 2008, when Clinton faced off against Obama in the Democratic primaries, she trafficked in the bitter racism that such structural inequities cement in the hearts of white Americans. From the *New York Times*:

> "I have a much broader base to build a winning coalition on," she said in [an] interview, citing an article by The Associated Press. "[It] found how Senator Obama's support among working, hard-working Americans, white Americans, is weakening again, and how whites in both states who had not completed college were supporting me. [. . .] These are the people you have to win if you're a Democrat in sufficient numbers to actually win the election. Everybody knows that."

Her call to bet on bigotry in order to win a Democratic election matters. Hillary Clinton has some relatively progressive ideas, including equal pay for women. Still, she claims to believe that health care is "a basic human right," while not fighting for true universal health care. She wholeheartedly supported welfare reform, also known as TANF, which not only proved to be harmful for many working-class black and Latino families, but also trafficked in lazy stereotypes about black and brown mothers.

Third-way politics, to which Clinton subscribes, is progressive on most social issues and to the right on most economic issues, reaffirming the capitalist structure that keeps people of color oppressed, while lulling some into believing that substantive progress is being made. Nothing about this necessarily makes Clinton a "worse" Democrat than her predecessors in a party that continues its slow slide to the right; it just undergirds my contention that both the Democratic Party and the Republican Party are the same on many issues that disproportionately affect people of color—*including* the women whom Clinton claims to champion.

Certainly, not all the women are white, and this brings us back to those blanket charges of sexism and how they fail to take into consideration the lived experiences of many women of color. What's funny—and not "funny ha-ha"—is how some white feminists who ride for Clinton as hard as Bernie bros ride for Sanders have been silent about the criminalization, sexual assault, and police brutality that black women and girls face. Despite this, they expect us now to be all sister suffrage—"Vote for women!"—or risk being deemed traitors to gender equality.

Cocooned in the white privilege that many of them deny, this type of white feminist expects black feminists with legitimate concerns to push those concerns aside for the so-called greater good—a good, to paraphrase both Harriet Tubman and Viola Davis, that exists over a line where there are "green fields and lovely flowers and beautiful white women with their arms stretched out to us . . . but we can't seem to get there no-how. We can't seem to get over that line."

Be clear: HRC has faced and continues to face extreme sexism. The misogyny is palpable. If she were a man, she would be finishing her second term and prepping for the Supreme Court by now. She can run with the big dogs and win because women know how to get it done. What exactly she'll get done, however, is up for debate.

So I say this without centering Bill Clinton's presidency—even though she played a critical role in his administration, which is just one part of her political career. I say this without talking about *his* morals or her hair or her "cankles," or her penchant for pantsuits, because anyone who does that will do it to any woman, at any time, from corporate America to the corners of America. I say this without insisting that she needs to smile more or be more approachable, less formidable or less intimidating: *"Abuela" Clinton has some issues that screaming "sexism" just won't fix.*

And there are ills within the Democratic Party that evoking the GOP bogeyman just won't cure. I get it; it is terrifying. This good-cop, bad-cop routine that Republicans and Democrats have perfected is convincing. But we will never really break this system—because it's not broken; it's working exactly as intended—if we allow our votes to be held hostage by identity politics and cosmetic diversity. There are questions that we need to ask ourselves, hard questions that we need to be free to ask our elected officials, without apology or caveats.

- Is black unemployment high and are black business opportunities low? Yes.
- Are incarceration rates high? Yes.
- Is reproductive-health-care access severely restricted for low-income women of color, particularly in the rural South? Yes.
- Is the privatization and tokenizing of education that allows for the closure of public schools around the country making it harder for low-income students of color to receive a competitive education? Yes.
- Are police officers killing and raping us? Yes.
- Are our children being subjected to poisoned water? Yes.

And that's just a sample questionnaire. I've heard a lot of "indict the system" black revolutionaries and so-called allies say, "If we don't vote Democrat, a Republican will be in office and Armageddon will be upon us." Well, Armageddon is already here, and this Democrat-or-GOP, lesser-of-two-evils seesaw has done nothing but make us dizzy.

So how do we stop it? I don't know, but I do know that my ancestors didn't march and martyr themselves for me to be held hostage by my vote simply because a woman is running for office, a woman who not only actively participated in laying the groundwork for some of these conditions but has also not convinced me that she is sincere in her claims that she will fight Congress for policies to rectify them. If that makes me a bad feminist, so be it.

I refuse to let them strangle my belief in the improbable—an America in which black women and the people we love are no longer targets trapped in the crosshairs of a weaponized political system—just so a woman can walk through the doors of 1600 Pennsylvania Avenue as commander in chief, as powerful and poetic as that may seem on the surface.

Feminism at the Polls

Liza Featherstone

Liza Featherstone is an American journalist and journalism professor who writes frequently on labor and student activism. "Feminism at the Polls" appeared in Dissent *magazine in the Summer 2016 issue.*

For the nation's handful of socialist feminists, the US presidential primary season is usually less inspiring than a ribbon cutting for our local Walmart. Usually we choose from a lineup of dutiful manservants of American-style capitalism, trying womanfully to convince ourselves that there are subtle differences between them. Maybe one has expressed a concern about poverty? Or perhaps he is black? Maybe he has a pretty cool wife? If so, we'll make a strenuous effort to prefer him over the others.

Most years, we hear no talk of serious redistribution, socialized medicine, or free higher education—policies embraced around the globe—and little about any issue specifically affecting women, other than abortion. We are thrilled if, in a debate, anyone asks these largely indistinguishable chaps about the pay gap between men and women.

Meanwhile, we try in vain to ignore the carnival of buncombe that is the Republican primary, hoping that our most conservative fellow citizens will have the sense to choose their nominee from among the 59 percent of Americans who are aware that dinosaurs and people did not walk the earth at the same time. This election has abruptly flipped that script.

The Republican primary has been surreal, pitting a misogynist reality TV star seething with sexual violence—that is even directed at other Republican males, such as when he boasted that he could have induced a former GOP candidate to "drop to [his] knees" for his endorsement—against a Tea Partier whose evangelically informed conservatism makes him an even worse choice for most female voters.

Yet the primary season's most startling facet has been the sudden salience of both socialism and feminism. Vermont senator Bernie Sanders is running as a self-identified "democratic socialist"—a historic first for a serious Democratic primary effort—while former secretary of state Hillary Clinton is poised to become the first woman president, running openly as a feminist. In this race, two movements crucial to human liberation—but too often absent from mainstream politics—abruptly took center stage in American public discourse, often clashing noisily. The cacophony revealed the fault lines of both establishment feminism and the socialist left. It also suggested sizable constituencies for both movements, and some hopeful ways to build them.

Too often, the choice between the two front-runners in the 2016 Democratic primary has been framed as a choice between feminism and socialism. The media has enjoyed and perpetuated this dichotomy. Some feminists—including Sady Doyle, Rebecca Traister, and Joan Walsh—claimed that although their politics were to the left of Hillary's, they were #withher because she was the feminist choice. Even some socialist feminists—like Suzanna Danuta Walters and Katha Pollitt, both writing in *The Nation*—prominently and publicly chose Clinton. To Pollitt, it mattered that Clinton was running as a feminist. Walters's piece was provocatively titled "Why This Socialist Feminist Is for Hillary," yet she gave no socialist reasons for her choice, instead deploying her "red-diaper baby" background as a kind of identity politics clickbait, the way a Log Cabin Republican renders his conventional politics noteworthy with his gayness.

For those of us who believe, for both practical and idealistic reasons, that socialism and feminism are inseparable, the notion that we had to choose between the two was exhaustingly absurd. But we were not necessarily surprised by this framing, or at least we shouldn't have been. The economic left—whether "socialist," social democratic, or simply progressive—never does a good enough job of explaining why its policy ideas are feminist. And mainstream feminism, captured and nourished by narrow elite and short-term interests, rarely foregrounds the economic and social policies that the vast majority of women need if we are to enjoy anything close to equality with men.

Feminist engagement with national elections tends to revolve entirely around abortion rights. The discussion of that vital issue was more materialist than usual this year, going beyond crude, though accurate, evocations of the Republican "War on Women." Sanders's platform promised to guarantee reproductive rights as part of his single-payer health plan, and even Clinton spoke of repealing the Hyde Amendment, which restricts poor women from using federal funding for abortions. Yet we rarely heard reproductive rights discussed in the context of broader economic rights. As the feminist writer Maureen Tkacik has observed in an essay published in my anthology *False Choices*, the economic constraints on young women are barriers to a truly free consideration of the "choice" to have (or not to have) children. Neoliberal feminism is willing to assert the right not to have a child for sound economic reasons, as Tkacik suggests, but a more radical, expansive, and expensive feminism would assert, with equal force, the right to *have* one, with the economic security that motherhood demands. Such a vision was not discussed this primary season, but both Hillary Clinton and Bernie Sanders brought other women's issues into the conversation, like paid family leave and equal pay. This was highly welcome.

Yet with most national women's organizations and famous feminists supporting Clinton—from Gloria Steinem to Roxane Gay to Courtney Love—feminist conversation foregrounded the goal of electing a woman president. This often devolved into the exercise of defending the female candidate against perceived sexist slights. This narrative of grievance gave new meaning to the "micro" prefix in microaggression. When Sanders said in a debate that "all the shouting" on gun control would not resolve the issue, Clinton and her supporters fired up the feminist base with an accusation of chauvinism: see, a woman being emphatic is perceived as "shouting"! Incidents like these put left feminists in a curious position, in which many became weirdly protective of a person who has not been stopped by patriarchy from attaining a net worth of over $30 million, and is poised to attain the most powerful political office on earth.

No wonder, given that net worth, that despite the number of

female-headed households living under the poverty line, we heard from Clinton that Sanders's emphasis on inequality made him a "single issue" candidate, in contrast to his opponent's "intersectionality." It was nice to hear this word (normally confined to graduate seminars or social justice Twitter) in a national election. But what was her feminism intersecting with, exactly? It was hard to make sense of this rhetoric—after all, the number of ways that access to health care, education, higher-paying jobs, and wealth are intertwined with race and gender can't even be counted. Elite feminism simply presents the spectacle of a few women intersecting with money and power, almost by chance, the way you might hope, lacking a timetable, to catch a high-speed train.

Speaking of intersections, given the robust tradition of feminist antimilitarism, from Virginia Woolf to Malala Yousafzai, we also heard too little feminist critique of the record of the former secretary of state, who not only voted for the war in Iraq, but advocated a belligerent approach to Libya and Iran that contrasted sharply to that favored by President Obama and the rest of his administration. Clinton also, behind the scenes, assisted and gave cover to a right-wing coup against the democratically elected government of Honduras, as Belén Fernández and Greg Grandin have written, which has greatly increased rape and femicide in that country.

We need a mainstream feminism that understands the impact of economic and foreign policy on the majority of women's lives. In deciding who to endorse, the mainstream feminist organization EMILY's List only considers the gender of candidates and their position on abortion rights. In light of that explicit criteria, it made sense for EMILY's List to endorse Clinton. But the group was not alone: other national feminist groups also overwhelmingly endorsed the former secretary of state. That the feminist lens on electoral politics is so narrow speaks to the need for much louder socialist voices within the women's movement.

Only a few feminists interrogated the goal of electing a female president. Sarah Leonard was one, arguing in her *Nation* essay "Which Women Support Hillary (and Which Women Can't Afford To)" that female representation in politics does little for women workers when compared to the potentially broader impact of redistributive universal social welfare programs.

Despite this, the Sanders agenda was not framed as a feminist one nearly often enough, reflecting the need of the left to speak the language of feminism more fluently. We did sometimes hear that Sanders's support for raising the minimum wage to $15 was feminist, since the majority of low-wage workers are women. (Throughout the primary season, Sanders has supported the nationwide movement to raise the minimum wage to $15, while Clinton has made clear that $12 would be just fine.) But rarely in this primary did we hear that single-payer health care, vigorously opposed by Secretary Clinton and stalwartly supported by Senator Sanders, benefits women even more than men, as the feminist health advocacy group Our Bodies Ourselves pointed out in 2009. Women have higher medical debt, higher medical expenses, and are more likely to navigate the health-care system for dependents. In addition, research shows that the kind of social benefits Sanders advocates—universal and distributed through the state, rather than through work or marriage—should be part of any feminist agenda: they advance women's equality more than any other policy approach. Instead, our current system practically mandates jobs and husbands, major sources of women's oppression (as delightful as they can be) as the primary means through which women should receive these benefits. There was equally little framing of free, public four-year college tuition—supported by Senator Sanders and opposed by his opponent—as a feminist priority, even though the majority of college students are women and young women bear the majority of student debt held in this country.

Another problem was that some of the organizations with the most practical grassroots knowledge of the intersection of race, class, and gender are unions. But with the mainstream media in any case largely uninterested in labor, neither candidate was asked many questions about the possibilities for expanding workers' organizing opportunities. Both Sanders and Clinton joined Verizon strikers on the picket lines, but could have also discussed the critical role of unions in fighting race and sex discrimination in the workplace.

Nor was the impending collapse of public-sector unionism or the ongoing ideological and material assault on the nation's public school teachers framed as a feminist issue, though so many of these workers are women of color. The elite hostility to public-sector workers, while certainly rooted in a desire to pay lower taxes and fury that any group in the working class enjoys a modicum of bargaining power, also stems from racism and sexism, an assumption that black women couldn't possibly deserve decent pay or benefits, or the respect of professional status.

We can lament the missed opportunities of the 2016 primary, but we should also view its aftermath as an inspiring invitation for social-ist feminists to engage with electoral politics. We should be making arguments about why social-democratic priorities are feminist, and we should also be explaining why feminism is integral to—and not a dis-traction from—a broader progressive agenda.

One way to do that is to look to candidates who can speak about both socialism and feminism at once. This is far easier to do when running for offices other than the presidency. With women already building on the Sanders momentum to run for state and local offices as socialists, the potential for socialist-feminist electoral politics seems rich.

One of these candidates is Debbie Medina, a democratic socialist running for New York State Senate. Asked why women should be so-cialists, she told *The Nation*,

> Think about it. Who does capitalism neglect and ignore? Women. Capitalism has no use for a woman who wants decent housing at a decent rent. . . . How is rent control not a women's issue? How is the Fight for $15 not a women's issue?

More of us should follow her example and run for county commis-sioner, school board, community board, or whatever other avenues to state power are open.

But the political terrain is not set just by candidates; it is also molded by organizations. Socialist feminists should also join—or infiltrate—national feminist groups like NARAL and Planned Parenthood (and especially NOW, which has a much more democratic, grassroots structure), and push them to focus much more on the economic challenges that the majority of women face.

We must also change the labor movement. One of the few major unions—and one of the few national feminist organizations—supporting Sanders was National Nurses United (NNU), which has campaigned tirelessly for him. The Coalition of Immokalee Workers has also been campaigning for Sanders. Strengthening the reach of organizations like this, which represent women in large numbers and fight for socialist priorities, will help to reshape the electoral landscape in the future.

If the leaders of our major national labor unions continue to insist on shilling for the worst candidates the Democratic Party can spit out, we need to build more independent labor organizations like NNU that are able to bring knowledge of women's everyday economic struggles into electoral politics. It was disgraceful that so many unions representing mostly women workers—the American Federation of Teachers, the Service Employees International Union, to name just a couple—endorsed Clinton, a candidate whose record and agenda are so deeply at odds with their members' interests, whether we are examining her campaign against teachers' unions in Arkansas or her tenure on the board of Walmart, a company famous for illegal union-busting, low wages, and sex discrimination. It reflects the deep need for democratic reform—and socialist feminist education—within those organizations, and that must be part of our electoral agenda for the future.

What will also help is fighting on the issues that we consider critical to the socialist feminist agenda. The Fight for $15, for example, offers a beacon of hope. The movement to raise the minimum wage to $15 swept the nation and enjoyed some concrete victories during the primary. This transformed the notion of a $15-an-hour wage from a leftist ideal promulgated by a socialist city councilwoman in liberal Seattle, and largely assumed to be too threatening to business, into a tangible goal embraced by much of the mainstream Democratic Party. So by April, even Clinton was rushing to appear supportive of the Fight for $15, joining fellow centrist Democrat Andrew Cuomo at a rally and photo-op to celebrate signing it into law in New York. It's too easy to point out how cynical she is, and how fast she changed her tune. But the goal of left politics is to make left ideas so popular that the most mainstream politicians will support them, and Clinton's shift on the Fight for $15 shows how, by organizing, we can do just that.

It was a surprisingly hopeful season, in which we heard the words "socialism" and "feminism" a lot more than we could ever have expected. A couple of us even found ourselves saying the words together, publicly, in the same breath. The surprising popularity of both Bernie and Hillary has shown us that the time for feminism and socialism is now. Bringing them together, in our political practice and our thinking, is our next challenge.

Don't Call Clinton a Weak Candidate:
It Took Decades of Scheming to Beat Her

Rebecca Solnit

Rebecca Solnit writes on a variety of subjects, including the environ-
ment, politics, place, and art. "Don't Call Clinton a Weak Candidate"
appeared in The Guardian *on November 14, 2016.*

Sometimes I think I have never seen anyone as strong as Hillary Clinton. That doesn't mean that I like and admire everything about her.
I'm not here to argue about who she is, just to note what she did. I
watched her plow through opposition and attacks the likes of which no
other candidate has ever faced and still win the popular vote. To defeat
her it took an unholy cabal far beyond what Barack Obama faced when
he was the campaign of change, swimming with the tide of disgust
about the Bush administration. As the *New York Times* reported, "By
the time all the ballots are counted, she seems likely to be ahead by
more than 2m votes and more than 1.5 percentage points. She will
have won by a wider percentage margin than not only Al Gore in 2000
but also Richard Nixon in 1968 and John F. Kennedy in 1960."

You can flip that and see that Trump was such a weak candidate
it took decades of scheming and an extraordinary international roster
of powerful players to lay the groundwork that made his election possible. Defeating Clinton in the electoral college took the 2013 gutting
of the Voting Rights Act by Republican appointees to the Supreme
Court. It took vast Republican voter suppression laws and tactics set
in place over many years. It took voter intimidation at many polling

places. It took the long Republican campaign to blow up the boring bureaucratic irregularity of Clinton's use of a private e-mail server into a scandal that the media obediently picked up and reheated.

It took James Comey, the director of the FBI, using that faux-scandal and his power to stage a misleading smear attack on Clinton eleven days before the election in flagrant violation of the custom of avoiding such intervention for sixty days before an election. It took a compliant mainstream media running after his sabotage like a golden retriever chasing a tennis ball. It took decades of conservative attacks on the Clintons. Comey, incidentally, served as deputy GOP counsel to the Senate Whitewater committee, that fishing expedition that began with an investigation into a messy real estate deal in Arkansas before Bill Clinton's presidency and ended with a campaign to impeach him on charges related to completely unrelated sexual activities during his second term.

It took a nearly decade-long reality TV show, *The Apprentice*, to deify Trump's cruelty, sexism, racism, and narcissism as essential to success and power. As the feminist media critic Jennifer Pozner points out: "Everything Trump said and did was framed in a way to flatter him, and more importantly, flatter his worldview." The colossal info-mercial fictionalized the blundering, cheating businessman as an unqualified success and gave him a kind of brand recognition no other candidate had.

It took the full support of Fox News, whose CEO, Roger Ailes, was so committed to him that after leaving the company following allegations of decades of sexual harassment of employees, he joined the Trump campaign. It took the withdrawal of too many Americans from even that caliber of journalism into the partisan unreliability of faux-news sites and confirmation-bias bubbles of social media.

It took the mainstream media's quarter-century of failure to address climate change as the most important issue of our time. It took decades of most media outlets letting the fossil-fuel industry's propaganda arm create the false framework of two equally valid opinions rather than reporting the overwhelming scientific consensus and tremendous danger of climate change.

To stop Hillary Clinton it also took Julian Assange, using WikiLeaks as a tool of revenge, evidently considering his grudge against the

Democratic nominee important enough to try to aid the campaign of a climate-denying racist authoritarian. Assange now appears to have so close a relationship with Russia that he often appears on the state-funded TV channel and news site RT. He tweeted protests when Russian president Vladimir Putin's information was included in the Panama Papers hack and has been coy about where his leaked information on the Democratic National Committee came from.

Many intelligence experts say it came from Russian hackers, and Putin made it clear that he favored Trump's win. The day Comey dropped his bombshell, the *New York Times* ran a story reassuringly titled "Investigating Donald Trump, FBI Sees No Clear Link to Russia" with its own astounding, underplayed revelation buried inside: "Investigators, the officials said, have become increasingly confident, based on the evidence they have uncovered, that Russia's direct goal is not to support the election of Mr. Trump, as many Democrats have asserted, but rather to disrupt the integrity of the political system and undermine America's standing in the world more broadly."

And it took a shortsighted campaign of hatred on the left, an almost hysterical rage like nothing I have ever seen before about any public figure. Some uncritically picked up half-truths, outright fictions, and right-wing spin to feed their hate, and rejected anything that diluted the purity and focus of their fury, including larger questions about the other candidate and the fate of planet Earth. It was so extreme that in recent weeks I was attacked for posting anti-Trump news stories on social media by furious people who took the position that to be overtly anti-Trump was to be covertly pro-Clinton. If the perfect is the enemy of the good, whose friend is it? The greater of two evils?

A lot of people seemed to think the Sanders-Clinton primary ended the night Trump was elected. I saw that stuckness from climate activists, antiracist journalists, civil rights champions, and others who you might expect would have turned to face the clear and present danger of a Trump presidency. I heard, for example, much about Clinton's failure to address the Dakota pipeline adequately—which was true, and bad, but overshadowed by what we heard so little about: Trump's million dollars or so invested in the pipeline and the guarantee he would use presidential powers to push it and every pipeline like it through.

It's impossible to disconnect the seething, irrational emotionality from misogyny, and the misogyny continues. Since election night, I've been hearing too many men of the left go on and on about how Clinton was a weak candidate. I've wondered about that word "weak," not only because it is so often associated with women, but because what they're calling her weakness was their refusal to support her. It's as if they're saying, "They sent a pink lifeboat and we sent it back, because we wanted a blue lifeboat, and now we are very upset that people are drowning."

Or, as my brilliant friend Aruna d'Souza put it: "At some point soon we need to discuss whether Sanders would have been able to win, but helpful hint: today, it just sounds like you're saying: 'The Democrats should have cut into Trump's lead in the misogynist vote and the whitelash vote by running a white man.' Let's come to terms with the racism and the misogyny first, before analyzing the what-ifs—because otherwise we're just going to replicate it forever. And if you think that the angry antiestablishment vote won (hence Sanders would have fared better), let me remind you that patriarchy and white supremacy are the cornerstones of the Establishment."

I know that if Clinton had been elected there would not be terrified and weeping people of color all over the country, small children too afraid to go to school, a shocking spike in hate crimes, high school students with smashed dreams marching in cities across the country. I deplore some of Hillary Clinton's past actions and alignments and disagreed with plenty of her 2016 positions. I hoped to be fighting her for the next four years. But I recognize the profound differences between her and Trump on race, gender, immigration, and climate, and her extraordinary strength, tenacity, and courage in facing and nearly overcoming an astonishing array of obstacles to win the popular vote. Which reminds us that Trump has no mandate and sets before us some of the forces arrayed against us.

Part II

Sexism and Misogyny

Donald and Billy on the Bus

Lindy West

Lindy West is an American writer, feminist, fat acceptance movement activist, and film criticism editor. "Donald and Billy on the Bus" appeared in the New York Times *on October 8, 2016.*

It's Billy Bush's snickering that really gets to me. In the video from 2005, published Friday by the *Washington Post*, you can hear Mr. Bush (first cousin to George W.) wheezing ecstatically as Donald J. Trump brags, inadvertently into a hot mic, about sexually harassing and groping women. The pair, along with a passel of unidentified men, are on a bus en route to film an *Access Hollywood* segment with the actress Arianne Zucker.

Through the window of the bus, Mr. Bush seems to spot Ms. Zucker first, as she waits to greet them. "Sheesh," he blurts, breathless, telling Mr. Trump how hot "your girl" is. You can feel Mr. Bush's giddiness, a contact high, at getting to join a more powerful man in the oldest and most sacred of male bonding exercises: objectifying women.

Mr. Trump spies Ms. Zucker too. "Whoa!"

"Yes!" Mr. Bush grunts, Beavis-esque, "Yes, the Donald has scored!"

Of course, "the Donald" has not "scored." The Donald is on the NBC lot to shoot a guest appearance on *Days of Our Lives* at the behest of his employer to promote his reality show, *The Apprentice*, while *Access Hollywood* produces an accompanying puff piece. This is work within work within work. Mr. Bush is at work. Mr. Trump is at work. Ms. Zucker is at work, and not only is she not Mr. Trump's "girl," she is a complete stranger who is also on camera and being paid to smile.

"Heh heh heh," Mr. Bush snickers. "My man!"

Such has it always been: powerful men sorting women's bodies into property and trash and "good" guys, average guys, guys you know, guys you love, guys on the *Today* show, going along with it. Snickering. Licking a boot here and there, joining in if they're feeling especially bitter or transgressive or insecure or far from the cameras that day. Perhaps, at their most noble, staying silent. Never speaking up, because the social cost is too high. It's easier to leave that for the victims to bear. After all, they're used to it.

"I gotta use some Tic Tacs," Mr. Trump says, still inside the bus, "just in case I start kissing her. You know I'm automatically attracted to beautiful—I just start kissing them, it's like a magnet. Just kiss. I don't even wait. And when you're a star, they let you do it. You can do anything. Grab them by the pussy. You can do anything." Mr. Bush and the bus toadies laugh.

You can't "do anything," actually. This might be a challenging concept for someone running a campaign so socially retrograde it's practically medieval, but women are allowed to own property now. That includes our own bodies, whether you feel "automatically" entitled to pieces of us or not.

Every woman knows a version of Donald Trump. Most of us have known more of them than we can (or care to) recall. He's the boss who thinks you owe him something; the date who thinks that silence means "yes" and "no" means "try harder"; the stranger who thinks your body's mere existence constitutes an invitation to touch, take, own, and destroy. He's every deadbeat hookup, every narcissistic loser, every man who's ever tried to leverage power, money, fame, credibility, or physical strength to snap your boundaries like matchsticks. He is hot fear and cold dread and a pit in your stomach. He's the man who held you back, who never took you seriously, who treated you like nothing until you started to believe it, who raped you and told you it was your fault and whose daddy was a cop so who would believe you anyway?

Come on, women. You know this man. I can name the ones in my past—name yours and imagine each as president, with every woman's life in his care. Would you even trust him to watch your dog? (That's a trick question because *he would never do it*. His defining characteristic is that he does not care about you.)

When Mr. Trump tells Mr. Bush that he's "gotta use some Tic Tacs" just in case he cannot restrain himself from non-consensually affixing his perfectly round, gasping lamprey mouth over Ms. Zucker's, he is talking about sexually assaulting a co-worker. When he says he grabs women's genitals, he is talking about sexually assaulting anyone he feels like, at any time. Female Trump voters: it's fine if you've come to terms with not being a full human being in the eyes of your party, but what about your daughters? Is that the life you want for them? You want old men to grab their genitals? You want the president of the United States to go around grabbing genitals?

Mr. Trump is rape culture's blathering id, and Sunday night Hillary Clinton (who, no doubt, has just as many man-made scars as the rest of us) has to stand next to him on a stage, and remain unflappable as she's held to an astronomically higher standard, and pretend that he is her equal while his followers persist in howling that sexism is a feminist myth. While Mr. Trump boasts about sexual assault and vows to suppress disobedient media, cable news pundits spend their time taking a protractor to Mrs. Clinton's smile—a constant, churning, microanalysis of nothing.

Many people, well, many men, are expressing their disgust with Mr. Trump the only way they know how: by invoking their mothers and daughters and sisters—people, presumably, with the anatomy Mr. Trump feels free to assess and knead. Hillary Clinton has been showing us all year, and all her life, that, sure, women can be cherished if you want, but they also can be president.

Meanwhile, right-wing lawmakers are scrambling, sanctimonious and pathetic, to distance themselves from their own hideous progeny, clearly hoping to salvage some personal credibility and perhaps even save their party. But here is the thing, the big thing, that Paul D. Ryan and Reince Priebus and Mike Pence and all the spineless Billy Bushes of the world (and plenty of progressive men too, for that matter) don't understand: most of you are no better than Mr. Trump; you are just more subtle.

If you have spent your career brutalizing and dehumanizing women legislatively rather than personally, you are no better. If you were happy to overlook months of violent racism, xenophobia, transphobia, and Islamophobia from the Trump campaign, but now you're mad that he used a bad word and tried to sleep with another man's wife, you are no better. If you have derided and stigmatized identity politics in an effort to keep the marginalized from organizing, you are no better. If you snicker or say nothing while your fellow men behave like Donald Trump, you are no better. The truth is that all of you have failed women for generations, and you deserve to lose our votes.

At Least Six Women Have Accused Trump of Sexual Misconduct— How Many More Will Come Forward?

Joan Walsh

Joan Maureen Walsh was editor-at-large of Salon.com before becoming national affairs correspondent for The Nation and an MSNBC political analyst. "At Least Six Women Have Accused Trump of Sexual Misconduct—How Many More Will Come Forward?" appeared in The Nation on October 13, 2016.

Based on the year he spent shadowing Donald Trump for his book *The Art of the Deal*, ghostwriter Tony Schwartz says that the GOP nominee's attacks on others always contain an element of projection: his foes share the traits he has.

> Something I saw early on w/ Trump: most negative things he says about others are actually describing him. Read his tweets with that in mind
> —Tony Schwartz (@tonyschwartz) July 27, 2016

It's beginning to look like when Trump announced his campaign by attacking undocumented Mexican "rapists," and today insists former president Clinton is a "rapist" too, he has indeed been projecting.

At least six women have come forward to multiple news outlets in the last twenty-four hours accusing Trump of kissing, groping, or even attempting to, as Trump so crudely put it in the *Access Holly-wood* video that rocked his campaign, grab them "by the pussy." A stranger seated next to Trump on a first-class flight; a *People* magazine reporter; a twenty-two-year-old who worked for a real estate firm in Trump Tower; a bevy of beauty-pageant winners—it seems there may be enough Trump sexual-assault accusers that every news outlet will eventually have their own.

Wednesday also saw the revelation that Trump entered the dressing rooms of the Miss Teen USA pageant, according to five former competitors, surprising juvenile contestants in various states of undress. Trump had already been caught boasting on tape to Howard Stern about one great perk of his job as beauty pageant owner: getting to burst into dressing rooms to inspect his property. "You know, they're standing there with no clothes. . . . And you see these incredible-looking women, and so, I sort of get away with things like that."

Trump helped trigger the tsunami of accusations himself, by insisting that what he called "locker-room talk" on the *Access Hollywood* video was "just words," and categorically denying during Sunday's debate that he'd ever put his words into action. "I just wanted to punch the screen," seventy-four-year-old Jessica Leeds told the *New York Times*. More than thirty years ago, she told the paper, Trump had lifted the armrest between their first-class seats and begun to grope her breasts and force his hands between her legs. "He was like an octopus. His hands were everywhere," Leeds recalled. "It was an assault." And by insisting the nearly forty-year-old rape charge against Bill Clinton by Juanita Broaddrick must be believed—and, in fact, hosting Broaddrick and other Clinton accusers at Sunday's debate—Trump has made it hard for his campaign to demand the media ignore the never-prosecuted and in some cases decades-old charges against him.

Trump denied all of the allegations to the news organizations that reported them—and of course, in recent hours, on Twitter as well. "You are a disgusting human being," an "agitated" Trump told the female *New York Times* reporter who called him about the claims. On the following Thursday morning, Trump's lawyers sent the *New York Times* a letter demanding a retraction and an apology.

Dozens of GOP officeholders fled Trump when the *Access*

Hollywood video came out, but in the last few days, as the smoke seemed to clear, several flipped back to supporting the GOP nominee, most notably Senators Deb Fischer of Nebraska and John Thune of South Dakota. Will they now flip back? With twenty-six days before the election, how can any Republican but the most rock-ribbed right-wing Neanderthal continue to support the party's nominee?

We'll have to see. The prospect of several accusers a day coming out describing similar Trump assaults has to be devastating for party leaders, but it doesn't necessarily change the power equation as they've balanced it to date: the loudest, most passionate elements of the party's base have stood by their man thus far, and it's hard to see why these accusations would peel off many of them, given that Trump is blaming the revelations on the machinations of the evil Hillary Clinton campaign.

But Trump's disgusting audiotape lit up the wires of sexual assault hotlines in the last week. The notion that his boasting triggered his victims to come forward, in one case after thirty years, is believable to people who work with sexual-assault victims, who often blame themselves for somehow inviting the abuse.

"Like many women, I was ashamed and blamed myself for his transgression," *People* staff writer Natasha Stoynoff wrote. "I minimized it ('It's not like he *raped me* . . .'); I doubted my recollection and my reaction. I was afraid that a famous, powerful, wealthy man could and would discredit and destroy me, especially if I got his coveted *People* feature killed. 'I just want to forget it ever happened,' I insisted." But when she saw Trump deny putting his offensive words into action, she could no longer forget.

There is no sign the Trump campaign will be cowed by the new allegations. The GOP nominee is up to his nasty old tricks on Twitter, and campaign manager Steve Bannon, who has faced his own accusations of domestic violence and sexual harassment, promises that he'll turn "Bill Clinton into Bill Cosby," keeping up the campaign to brand the former president a rapist. Alex Jones's Infowars.com continues to challenge fans to disrupt Clinton campaign events by screaming and carrying signs calling Bill Clinton a rapist; on Wednesday two young white men were escorted from vice presidential nominee Tim

Kaine's rally at Davidson College outside Charlotte, North Carolina. This campaign is unlikely to rise from the gutter, on the GOP side, any time soon.

But as even Trump's defenders try to blame these latest allegations on the Clinton campaign, they ought to look in the mirror. On August 6, 2015, Fox News host Megyn Kelly tried to warn them of the baggage the first-time candidate carried, when it came to his treatment of women.

> You've called women you don't like fat pigs, dogs, slobs, and disgusting animals. . . . Your Twitter account has several disparaging comments about women's looks. You once told a contestant on *Celebrity Apprentice* it would be a pretty picture to see her on her knees. Does that sound to you like the temperament of a man we should elect as president, and how will you answer the charge from Hillary Clinton, who was likely to be the Democratic nominee, that you are part of the war on women?

Kelly was rewarded by a campaign of misogynist hate from Fox viewers led by Trump, who depicted her as a menstruating harridan with "blood coming out of her wherever." So you can't say you weren't warned, Republicans. This is on you. And a word to the media: given Trump's apparent ability to turn coarse, threatening words into action, maybe it's time to stop claiming that he really doesn't intend to forcibly deport eleven million undocumented people, or put Clinton in prison. The burden of proof that he's not a misogynist authoritarian is now officially on Donald Trump.

Why We Trust Donald Trump's Accusers but Didn't Believe Bill Clinton's

Caitlin Flanagan

Caitlin Flanagan is a former staff writer at the New Yorker *and a contributor to* The Atlantic. *"Why We Trust Donald Trump's Accusers but Didn't Believe Bill Clinton's" appeared in the* Washington Post *on October 14, 2016.*

When Donald Trump brought three women who have accused Bill Clinton of sexual misconduct to the second presidential debate, his aides said he had three goals. He wanted to throw Hillary Clinton off her game by putting them in her sightline (although the debate committee nixed his original plan to seat them in his VIP box). He wanted to remind voters that Bill Clinton's presidency had been marked by accusations far more serious than the acts Trump described to Billy Bush on the *Access Hollywood* bus. And he wanted to reinforce a central belief of the most energetic anti-Clinton forces: that Hillary was deeply complicit in the ruin of the women who accused her husband.

Never has a political strategy been so shortsighted. Within days, women began to come forward to accuse Trump of the acts he had described on the bus. It was only a matter of time before he turned to the next page of the low-life playbook: defending himself by implying that the women were too ugly for a man of his taste to grope. "Look at her," he said in disgust about *People* magazine reporter Natasha Stoynoff, who says he pushed her against a wall and forced his tongue into her mouth in 2005.

Trump is crass, bullying—and no dummy. Yes, he had all but invited women to come forward and accuse him. But by pairing his accusers with Bill Clinton's, he made us confront a potent reality: a man facing the allegations Clinton did might not be electable today.

When Clinton was confronting serious accusations of abuse, the country had a different attitude toward women who came forward with unverified (and often, unverifiable) accounts of sexual assault. Clinton's inner circle was able to dismiss the women—on the basis of their backgrounds and sexual history—as crazies or trailer trash; as the accusations piled up, adviser Betsey Wright coined the repugnant and resonant phrase "bimbo eruption." (Clinton employed the "nuts and sluts defense," as Patricia Ireland, then president of the National Organization for Women, eventually called the tactic.) What's more, these stories appeared within a larger and widely held belief system that women would readily lie about sexual assault for purposes of financial gain, romantic revenge, or mere attention.

The accusers then—like Trump's today—lacked witnesses, evidence, and immediate reporting to the authorities. Paula Jones says that while working as a $6.35-an-hour Arkansas state employee, she was summoned to the hotel room of Clinton, then the governor. She had hoped he wanted to discuss a promotion; instead, she says, he grabbed her, exposed himself to her, and propositioned her. Juanita Broaddrick says that while she was volunteering for one of his gubernatorial campaigns, he invited himself to her hotel room to discuss the work. Once there, she says, he violently raped her. Kathleen Willey says that when she visited Clinton in the Oval Office, he took her to a side room and groped her.

The Clinton defense strategy centered on blatantly misogynistic practices. Even progressive feminists and traditionally liberal late-night comics did their part to discredit and ridicule the women. In an act of proto-revenge porn, an ex-boyfriend of Jones sold private sexual photographs of her to *Penthouse* a few months after her claim became public. She was immediate fodder for harsh jokes, many focusing on her appearance. (Several years later, she capitalized on her notoriety by posing nude for the magazine, further marginalizing herself.) Today, there is far greater sympathy for women whose nude photographs are made public, as well as a gathering consensus that work in the sex industry does not delegitimize a claim of assault.

Willey's claim was disbelieved at the time, in part because she had once told a pal that she was sexually attracted to Clinton—and that she had voluntarily visited him a second time after he grabbed her. But we now understand that sexual assault can exist within a complex pattern of human behavior, and that no attitude or subsequent action of the woman excuses a criminal act.

Gloria Steinem's defense of Clinton is the most difficult to imagine taking place today. In 1998, she wrote in the *New York Times* that he had not assaulted Willey or Jones. Rather, she wrote, the fact that he had not raped either of them after they pushed him away was evidence that he "took 'no' for an answer." To combine the language of Trump (speaking to Billy Bush) with the philosophy of Steinem: it is okay for a man to move on a woman "like a bitch," so long as he doesn't force the sex act on her if she fights back.

Clinton and his defenders got away with this approach partly because he was a pro-choice progressive who fiercely defended the causes most important to feminists. But more than that, it was a different time, and something really has changed.

Consider, as one example among many, the public shaming of Nate Parker, the director of the new *Birth of a Nation*. He was accused of rape in 1999 while an undergraduate at Penn State. Unlike so many college men who are accused of rape, he went to trial, where he was found not guilty—which ought to be the gold standard for absolving oneself of an accusation of sexual misconduct. But he has never escaped the charges, which have shadowed the release and reception of his movie. Several of Bill Cosby's accusers have no witnesses and no evidence, and they have come forward many years after the events they say took place—yet we are willing to hear them out. College women, whose claims of rape by fellow students were for many years interpreted as a natural consequence of the sexual revolution, are now taken seriously as crime victims.

Trump's defenses—advanced, as were Clinton's, by his surrogates—have been straight out of Little Rock. The women are said to be politically motivated (Joe Scarborough: They're part of a calculated

"October surprise"); attention hungry (Ben Carson: The media has told them, "Look, if you're willing to come out and say something, we'll give you fame"); liars (Trump spokeswoman Katrina Pierson on Jessica Leeds's claim that Trump groped her after lifting the armrest between their airplane seats: "First-class seats have fixed armrests"). This way of treating accusers used to work, but it doesn't anymore. Even Bill Clinton would have to find a different tack. Yet unlike with Clinton's accusers, who have no more or less proof of their accounts than do Trump's, this time the public seems more inclined to believe.

The nature of culture is progressive and cumulative. In 1987, Judge Douglas H. Ginsburg's nomination to the Supreme Court was rejected because he admitted to having smoked pot as a law professor at Harvard. Today we have a president whose high school yearbook attests to his high times and whose memoir describes his having done "blow" as a rootless young college graduate. And what was once an acceptable way to treat women who come forward with stories like Jones's or Broaddrick's is acceptable no longer. At long last—far too late and just in time—something has changed.

Hillary Clinton Has One More Badly Behaved Man Left to Vanquish

Katha Pollitt

Katha Pollitt is a columnist for The Nation *and the author of four essay collections and two books of poetry. "Hillary Clinton Has One More Badly Behaved Man Left to Vanquish" appeared in* The Nation *on November 2, 2016.*

As in some ancient myth, Hillary Clinton, warrior princess, could only succeed in her quest for the kingdom by vanquishing Phallus, the many-headed god of male sexual craziness. First she had to defeat the ghost of Bill Clinton, and that wasn't so hard because Bill was a popular politician even when his sins were fresh in the public memory; now he was old and his sins were too. Then there was the giant, Donald of the tiny hands, and he helped vanquish himself by being too gross and proud of it even for many in his own party. It was all going so well—her campaign was even thinking of venturing into seriously red places like Arizona just for the heck of it—when, a mere eleven days before the election, up popped a ridiculous troll: Anthony Weiner, the irrepressible dick-pic-sending long-disgraced estranged husband of Huma Abedin, Hillary's aide and friend. For some reason, Abedin and Weiner may have shared a laptop, on which there may have been both Weiner's sexts, possibly to an underage girl in North Carolina, and e-mails to or from Abedin that may have something to do with Hillary's State Department correspondence. We know all this because James Comey, the Republican who heads the FBI, ignored Department of Justice protocol and told Congress he was investigating the matter, although he was unable to say what the matter was or when he would know. By the time you read this, the whole thing may have blown over. Or not. Meanwhile, what have we learned so far?

1. If you are a woman in politics, don't get married.
2. If you are a married woman in politics, get a divorce. Better still, become a widow. All the perks of marriage and none of the risks.
3. Whether or not you are in politics, do not share a laptop with your husband, especially if he is a pervert. Believe me, you don't want to know!
4. If you are a Democratic president, do not give important jobs to Republicans, especially jobs having to do with manly stuff like law, order, war, and guns. You won't win brownie points with the opposition; you'll only reinforce the notion that Democrats are girly men.

I'm not the only person to have noticed that the campaign of the first woman to run for president from a major party has ended up being all about men behaving badly. Just look at Trump's campaign: former campaign manager Corey Lewandowski, accused of manhandling a woman reporter at a rally in March; the unspeakable Roger Ailes, forced out as head of Fox News after multiple women came forward with credible charges of harassment and abuse, now a campaign adviser; Breitbart chairman Stephen Bannon, the current campaign CEO, charged with domestic violence in 1996; surrogates Rudy Giuliani and Newt Gingrich, proud adulterers and huge hypocrites. It's as if hating women, being accused of sex crimes, and being a terrible husband are job qualifications. (And maybe that's not the only place it's a plus on your résumé: after he left the Trump campaign, CNN snapped Lewandowski right up). But then this is Trump, who boasted about the size of his penis in a primary debate, which has to be a first. Could the clouds of testosterone billowing from the campaign have something to do with the fact that Trump is facing a woman? Just don't forget who has the dick around here, people! Don't forget who is the grabber and who is the pussy!

It might comfort Hillary Clinton to remember that she is not the first woman politician to have had career trouble because of the men in her life when she got too close to the White House. In 1984, Geraldine Ferraro, Walter Mondale's running mate and the first woman vice presidential candidate from a major party, faced an investigation by a House ethics panel stemming from complaints made by the Washington Legal Foundation, a right-wing legal organization, that she had violated a congressional ethics law by not disclosing her husband's financial information. The inquiry revealed that Ferraro had more money than her regular-Queens-mom image suggested—she wasn't just a dumb housewife who somehow got into Congress; she was a rich dumb housewife. (After the election, the committee found that while she had indeed violated the law, she had done so unintentionally, and, noting that other members of the House had acted similarly, recommended no censure.) Her campaign was scandalized again when news broke that one of her husband's companies had rented out space to a porn distributor. (This was before porn was cool.) And then there were the usual misogynist slurs and crudities: Ferraro was ambitious and unqualified, a man-hater and a criminal. Barbara Bush called her "rhymes with rich" and George H.W. Bush, her vice presidential opponent, boasted after a debate that he had "kicked a little ass." The all-male Catholic hierarchy treated her with contempt: unlike her fellow pro-choice Catholic Mario Cuomo, she was pointedly not invited to the Al Smith dinner when her running mate couldn't attend.

Since this is my last column before the election, I'm trying mightily to wring something positive out of the sorry fact that in 2016, one candidate is an open enemy of women's rights and progress and is currently winning the support of a majority of white male voters. Maybe we've seen so much sexism because the truth is out: as antifeminists always feared, women really are men's equal. The phallus is all men have, so they have to wave it whenever they can. Trump the bitch! Hillary has everything a male pol is supposed to have: brains, experience, money, organization, devoted followers, a thick skin, and, yes, stamina. Furthermore, she's not the only woman who can make that claim. It's harder these days to dismiss a woman by suggesting she's ignorant of policy and lacks credentials. So, suddenly, policy is boring, credentials are boring—as so often happens, when women get something, it no longer matters. But power always matters. That's what Phallus and his sidekicks are afraid of. Go, warrior princess!

Part III

Women and Governance

What Wendy Davis Stood For

Amy Davidson

Amy Davidson is a staff writer at the New Yorker. *"What Wendy Davis Stood For" appeared in the* New Yorker *on June 26, 2013.*

"Something special is happening in Austin tonight," Barack Obama tweeted late Tuesday, with the hashtag #StandWithWendy. That is Wendy Davis, a Texas state senator who, at that point, had been standing on the floor of the legislature for more than nine hours—talking about women's bodies, their health, their lives—and would stand for about four more before Republicans, amid shouting and with brazenly dubious parliamentary tactics, forced an end to her filibuster. By then, though, she had won both a temporary and a long-term victory: a bill that would have left only five abortion clinics in the 260,000 square miles of Texas failed, even though Republicans first tried to pretend that it hadn't. They'll get another chance. But Davis reminded everyone that despite the steady dismantling of abortion rights in state legislatures, it's possible to fight back. People might yell at you on the floor and for you from the rafters, and you might, if only for the moment, win.

Davis had started her filibuster at about eleven a.m. The antiabortion-rights bill would have banned the procedure after twenty weeks and placed conditions on clinics—for equipment, for admitting privileges for doctors at hospitals within thirty miles—that would have made it impossible for them to stay open. The best guess, looking at a map, was that some women in Texas would end up driving over the Mexican border, and others might end up in some back room. But the bill had to pass by midnight, when the session ended. And so Davis set out to talk until the next day.

What did she talk about? What the bill really meant. What towns and the women who lived in them would lose; how a pregnancy unfolded—all points on which, she noted, her male colleagues seemed vague. "Lawmakers, either get out of the vagina business or go to medical school," Davis said. Davis is fifty. She had a child when she was nineteen. She went to law school at Harvard. She wore a pale skirt and jacket. And in the hours she spoke she read the stories of people who had testified about the bill. According to the *Texas Tribune*'s live blog, at one point she cried, reading the testimony of one of the bill's opponents, a woman who had needed to seek an abortion after twenty weeks because of unexpected medical complications.

Davis almost made it past midnight. She couldn't sit down or take a break for the bathroom, and if she got help or went off-topic more than three times the filibuster would be over too. That last was tricky, not because her plan had been to read the Federalist Papers or every volume of Harry Potter out loud but because at about ten p.m. the Republicans controlling the state senate tried to claim that her mentions of the Planned Parenthood budget and an earlier bill requiring sonograms before abortions were somehow not "germane," and that that and a colleague helping her with a back brace meant that she was done. Her Democratic colleagues disagreed, loudly. What followed has been widely described as chaos—a "ruckus," the Republican lieutenant general David Dewhurst said, caused by "an unruly mob." Davis kept standing, in pink-and-lime sneakers.

And by then, people across the country kept watching. The president himself wasn't tweeting about Davis, exactly—@BarackObama is the account of Organizing for Action, which works for his agenda (and for whom he does sign tweets). But there were enough eyes on Texas that what the Republicans tried to do next—passing the bill after midnight, without making it clear what measure was being voted on, and then claiming that the vote had gone through before time was up—didn't work. And Wendy Davis won.

How Can We Get More Women in Elected Office? Look to New Hampshire

Rebecca Hellmich

Rebecca Hellmich is a communications and advocacy fellow at Fair-Vote. "How Can We Get More Women in Elected Office? Look to New Hampshire" appeared in In These Times *on November 4, 2014.*

The people of New Hampshire take great pride in holding the nation's first presidential primary every four years. But the Granite State has a new claim to fame: its number of women in elected office.

As reported after the 2012 elections in *Bloomberg Businessweek*, New Hampshire became the first state in the US "to put female politicians in control of the governor's office and the entire congressional delegation." Over the course of American history, men have usually been in that position—women first won a congressional or gubernatorial election less than a century ago, and even today, Iowa and Mississippi have never elected a single woman to those offices.

But after the 2012 election, in which Maggie Hassan won an open-seat election for governor and two women swept the US House races to join two previously elected female US senators, New Hampshire became the first state to reverse that historic norm. Today, New Hampshire women hold those seats as well as the office of mayor in two of the state's five largest cities. Moreover, just over a third of state legislators are women, placing New Hampshire fifth in the country for state legislative representation.

Earlier this year, Representation 2020 released the first of its annual

State of Women's Representation reports, featuring the organization's Gender Parity Index (GPI). Defining parity as "the point at which women and men are just as likely to hold elected office," the GPI establishes parity scores on a scale from zero to 100 for how well women are represented in elections for governor, US Congress, and other major city and statewide offices. A gender parity score (GPS) of 50 indicates that a state has reached gender parity.

After the 1992 elections, the national median GPS was 9.8. That median has crept up to 15.9, with eight states still lagging in single digits, trailed by Virginia with a GPS of only 4.5. "The Gender Parity Index," explains Representation 2020 project director Cynthia Terrell, "allows us to measure trends within and among states over time. It shows us just how far we have to go, especially when we look at elections for executive offices like governor and mayor, where growth of women's representation is particularly stagnant."

Due to its outstanding performance in 2012, New Hampshire achieved the highest-ever Gender Parity Score of 47.5. This week, New Hampshire is poised to make gender parity history again. Male candidates are running strong challenges to Governor Hassan, Senator Jeanne Shaheen, and Representative Carol Shea-Porter. But given the weight the Gender Parity Index gives to the office of governor and to recent elections for governor and Congress, Hassan's reelection will likely result in New Hampshire becoming the first state to cross the 50.0 GPS threshold and achieve gender parity in elected office.

After the 2012 elections, one journalist described the synchronicity of factors that went into the election of the nation's first all-female delegation as "a perfect storm." The question is, how was this "perfect storm" of gender parity achieved, and how can New Hampshire maintain it?

INGREDIENTS FOR GENDER PARITY IN NEW HAMPSHIRE'S ELECTED OFFICES

New Hampshire has a history of women candidates doing better in the state legislature than in most states. As long ago as the mid-1980s, women held more than a third of the seats, and it's never dipped below 25 percent since—even as women have yet to reach that percentage of state legislative seats nationally. In 2008, the state's senate became the nation's first to have majority women, with thirteen of twenty-four seats held by women. (That share of seats has now dropped to nine of twenty-four.) Such success stories, however, are quite new for federal offices. In fact, the first woman to win an election for US Congress in New Hampshire, Representative Shea-Porter, was only elected in 2006.

In the following years, women took New Hampshire state and federal elections by storm, including wins for both US Senate seats: Democrat Jeanne Shaheen (who also served as the state's second female governor from 1997 to 2003) in 2008 and Republican Kelly Ayotte (who had been appointed as the state's attorney general in 2004) in 2010. In 2012, Maggie Hassan became New Hampshire's third female governor, Ann McLane Kuster regained the second US House seat, and the first ever all-female congressional delegation in US history was created.

When it comes to understanding the history of female representation in the state, it starts with the House. New Hampshire's lower house has one distinct characteristic, often referenced when the issue of gender parity comes up: its size. The House of Representatives has four hundred members, making it the largest individual chamber in the nation despite the state's relatively small size. The House also uses a system in which districts can vary greatly in population, ranging from single-winner districts where only one member is elected, to multi-winner districts where up to eleven members are elected (thus more than one candidate "wins" the election).

Many researchers suggest that multi-winner districts increase the chances of women being recruited to run and to win. Voters also seem to factor in voting for women differently when given the chance to vote for more than one seat. In the 2012 election, for example, every one of the six Democrats able to win in multi-winner districts electing more than five representatives was a woman, edging out Republican men in each case. These unique parts of New Hampshire's electoral structure present more opportunities for women to run and get elected in the first place, creating a pipeline for higher office. They also provide a state government with more local engagement.

"You have a high level of engagement and a high level of communication with your legislature because of the size, because of multimember districts, because there's four hundred others in the lower house," says Erin Vilardi, director of the national nonpartisan organization Vote Run Lead. "You've got people that you're really accessible to. That creates a really healthy democracy inside New Hampshire." Raymond Buckley, the chairman of the New Hampshire Democratic Party, suggests that New Hampshire's political parties contribute to the state's legacy as a gender parity leader. "State parties can, and in the case of the NHDP do, play a role in encouraging women to hold positions of leadership and responsibility at every level. Women hold four of the six positions on the Democratic National Committee from New Hampshire."

The state legislature is also a part-time job, to the point of essentially being a volunteer position. Salaries are on the lower end of the spectrum ($200 per two-year term) when compared to other states, like California, where legislators can make upwards of $90,000 per year.

Some theorize that this has encouraged women to run because it contributes to turnover and fewer men seeing it as a long-term job. Governor Hassan observed in a *BuzzFeed* interview, "The fact that a New Hampshire legislator's position is not seen as a career or a way of supporting a family has meant that it draws women."

While this may help create chances for older women able to afford to serve without compensation, it also might create barriers for young women, who are important for a state's pipeline to higher office. None of the New Hampshire women serving in Congress or as a governor started their careers in the House.

There seems to be a "strong tradition of women supporting other women" in New Hampshire, says Clare Bresnahan, program director of She Should Run, a sister organization of the Women's Campaign Fund. "The idea of role models—to be able to see so many women in New Hampshire politics become the norm, and then you're also getting that actual mentorship and sponsorship—is invaluable but also hard to quantify. But it's incredibly important to how the women have come up through the ranks in New Hampshire."

The experiences of the current trailblazing female delegation are certainly reflective of this: former New Hampshire senator Susan McLane mentored and encouraged her daughter, Ann "Annie" McLane Kuster (who now serves as congresswoman) and Jeanne

Shaheen when she was the state's second female governor (now serving as senator). Shaheen now mentors Governor Hassan. Vilardi suggests that this kind of mentorship, complemented with the existence of recruitment groups like Emerge Vermont, has led to a generational, almost cyclical, development and cultivation of women politicians in the state.

As Kuster puts it: "The first generation of women in politics were widows of politicians, and the next generation were wives and daughters. In this group, it's very apparent that three of us are lawyers, one was a teacher, and one was a social worker. We're working mothers. We're the next generation." Buckley agrees that female mentorship plays a role in getting women elected, especially for the current delegation. He also points out that women can actually have a slight advantage in New Hampshire.

"This is a relatively new phenomenon," Buckley says. "When all things are equal, women have a slight advantage with NH voters. It is also clear that women have recruited, promoted, and appointed other women bringing them into the process." The ingredients and the recipe for New Hampshire's gender parity legacy are clearly working—and observers on the national level are taking note. Case in point: when asked what woman politician she admired (besides Hillary Clinton) in a recent *Politico* segment, Meghan McCain's answer was New Hampshire's Senator Ayotte.

"She does what my dad used to do [when I was] growing up. It's a reverse—her husband stays at home in New Hampshire, while she goes to the Senate and works," McCain said. "And it never even occurred to me that that was a possibility, as terrible as that is. And it's like the first woman that I have ever talked to that I was like: This is real—this is feminism."

REMAINING WORK TO DO

Still, gender politics in New Hampshire are far from ideal. Last month, state representative Steve Vaillancourt wrote a post on a blog called *NH Insider*. After warning readers in bold letters at the top that the material might "prove uncomfortable" and providing the caveat "I don't plan to say anything really offensive here," he compared the physical appearances of state representative Marilinda Garcia and

Congresswoman Ann McLane Kuster, both vying for New Hampshire's second congressional district.

"Let's be honest," Vaillancourt wrote. "Does anyone not believe that Congressman Annie Kuster is as ugly as sin? And I hope I haven't offended sin." Garcia, in contrast, is "one of the most attractive women on the political scene anywhere."

Vaillancourt's reasoning was based on "some polling data which went by too fast for me to write down," and it was necessary to discuss because "if we stop to admit it, looks matter in politics." His comments, as well as his surprise when many responded with outrage, illustrate that, despite New Hampshire's record as a gender parity leader, the state has a long way to go toward eliminating sexism in politics. "Even in a state where there are a lot more women in office," Bresnahan says, "they still face those really outdated stereotypes and sexist comments from opponents or from folks in the media." How then can New Hampshire continue to encourage gender parity amidst attitudes like Vaillancourt's?

The first item of business, Bresnahan says, should be for female politicians to continue to call out and address such sexist commentaries: "It is essential that for women in office they continue to, as Carol Shea-Porter says: Name it, change it, and shame it." Vilardi suggests that continuing the use of multimember districts and instituting other fair voting methods that increase women's chances for running and winning elected offices would go a long way as well, and emphasizes the importance of having built-in accountability for these systems: "We need the parties, we need entities encouraging women to run."

Women Actually Do Govern Differently

Claire Miller

Claire Cain Miller is a correspondent for the New York Times, *where she writes about gender, families, and the future of work for* The Upshot, *a* Times *site for analysis of policy and economics. "Women Actually Do Govern Differently" appeared in the* New York Times *on November 10, 2016.*

Fed up with the government shutdown in 2013, Senator Susan Collins took the floor, presented a three-point plan, and implored colleagues on both sides of the aisle to work with her. As soon as she walked off, her phone rang. The first senators to call her, she said, were women: Kelly Ayotte and Lisa Murkowski, fellow Republicans, and Amy Klobuchar, a Democrat.

"I've always thought that was significant," said Ms. Collins, a Republican from Maine. "And indeed, we put together a plan for the reopening of government, and women led the way."

Tuesday failed to be a ceiling-shattering day for women in government. In addition to Hillary Clinton's loss, the number of female governors dropped to five from six, according to the Center for American Women and Politics at Rutgers. Kate Brown of Oregon was the only woman to win a governor's race. The number of women in Congress stayed flat at 104, or 19 percent of seats. (The Senate had a net gain of one woman and the House a net loss of one.) Thirteen states will send no women to the 115th Congress, including Mississippi and Vermont, which have never had a woman in Congress.

Women's representation in government is stalled, and in some cases moving backward. Does that make a difference to the work of governing? Yes, according to decades of data from around the world. Women govern differently than men do in some important ways. They tend to be more collaborative and bipartisan. They push for far more policies meant to support women, children, social welfare, and—when they're in executive positions—national security. But these bills are also more likely to die, research shows, largely because of gender bias.

Women in Congress sponsor and co-sponsor more bills than men do, and bring 9 percent more federal money to their districts, according to a study in the *American Journal of Political Science*. Those bills are more likely to benefit women and children or address issues like education, health, and poverty. In Congress, for instance, women fought for women's health coverage in the Affordable Care Act, sexual harassment rules in the military, the inclusion of women in medical trials, and child-care vouchers in welfare overhauls.

"All members of Congress have to follow their constituency, but because of their personal experiences either as women in the workforce or as mothers, they might be inclined to legislate on some of these issues," said Michele L. Swers, a professor of government at Georgetown University who studies gender and policymaking.

In a new analysis of the 151,824 public bills introduced in the House between 1973 and 2014, to be published in *Political Science Research and Methods*, researchers found that women were significantly more likely than men to sponsor bills in areas like civil rights, health, and education. Men were more likely to sponsor bills in agriculture, energy, and macroeconomics. An analysis of floor speeches during the 106th Congress, by political scientists at the University of Iowa and Oklahoma State University, found that women spent more time talking about policy concerns like women's health and family issues. Another study, of State of the State speeches from 2006 to 2008 published in *State and Local Government Review*, found that female governors devoted much more attention to social welfare issues than male governors did, even after controlling for political and situational factors.

Women are less likely to vote for war or the death penalty. Women's representation in legislatures is significantly correlated with the abolition of capital punishment, according to a study of 125 countries published in July by researchers at Sul Ross State University in Texas. A higher share of female legislators correlates with less military spending and less use of force in foreign policy, even after controlling for other explanations like partisanship, according to an analysis by researchers from Texas A&M University of data from twenty-two established democracies from 1970 to 2000.

Yet when women are in executive positions, the opposite is true: they are more hawkish than men. The researchers said that could be in part because of a need to overcome stereotypes of women as weak. Margaret Thatcher, Golda Meir, and Indira Gandhi, all of whom governed in conflicts, were described as governing like men.

Whether women's policies become law is another question. Studies show they hit more obstacles than men's policies.

Over all, female lawmakers are just as successful as men at getting their bills passed—except when the bills are about issues affecting women, health, education, and social welfare, according to a new study of four decades of House bills by Craig Volden of the University of Virginia, Alan E. Wiseman of Vanderbilt University, and Dana E. Wittmer of Colorado College.

Then, only 1 percent of bills sponsored by women passed, compared with 4 percent of all bills. That has been true since 1970, even when controlling for other factors that influence bills' success. The researchers concluded that it was not because of a gender difference in expertise or lawmaking ability, but because of institutional bias. Bills on the issues that women dominate are often gridlocked in committee, so they never make it to a vote.

"These are highly contentious issues in the first place, and it could be because there are relatively fewer women in Congress and as committee chairs, they might have less of a built-in coalition to push these through," Mr. Wiseman said.

Yet women also have advantages in governing—and the biggest gender differences appear during behind-the-scenes work. A variety of research has found that women interrupt less (but are interrupted more), pay closer attention to other people's nonverbal cues, and use a more democratic leadership style compared with men's more autocratic style. The result is that women build coalitions and reach consensus more quickly, researchers say.

"Women share their power more; men guard their power," said

Michael A. Genovese, director of the Institute for Leadership Studies at Loyola Marymount University, who has studied gender and leadership.

Senator Kirsten E. Gillibrand, Democrat of New York, said the data backs up her experience in the Senate. "Women tend to be less partisan, more collaborative, listen better, find common ground," she said. "Every time I've had a bill that's important to me, I've had strong Republican women helping me pass it." These days, partisanship can seem more highly valued than collaboration in Washington, and without more women entering government, their influence might be muted.

"Women have the great potential to govern differently," said Lyn Kathlene, a political scientist who studied gender and governing and is now director of Spark Policy Institute. "But my expectation is that's going to be less overt than behind the scenes, because the reality is you have to play the game as the game's played."

The Senate Bathroom Angle

Gail Collins

Gail Collins is an op-ed columnist at the New York Times. *"The Senate Bathroom Angle" appeared in the* New York Times *on December 22, 2016.*

We are sorely in need of some cheerful news out of Washington, so I'm going to tell you Barbara Mikulski's story about the Senate bathrooms. Almost every veteran woman legislator, in every level of government, has a story about the shortage of bathroom facilities at work. Really, there needs to be a book on this. It could have a happy ending, and none of the chapters would involve Russian attempts to manipulate an election.

Mikulski, eighty, has served in Congress longer than any other woman in history. She's retiring this month after representing Maryland for thirty years in the Senate. Before that she spent ten years in the House. She was a social worker who got into Democratic politics during a battle to stop a planned highway that was threatening the ethnic Baltimore neighborhoods she loved. It was an unusual career route at the time, but she was an unusual person. "One of the things they said was that I didn't look the part . . ." Mikulski, who is four-foot-eleven, recalled. "You know, chunky and I have a definite blue-collar style, so I wasn't to the manner born, to the trust fund inherited."

The classic way for a woman to win a seat in the Senate was to follow a famous male relative. Many of her predecessors were widows who succeeded their husbands. Though Nancy Kassebaum, the daughter of Republican presidential candidate Alf Landon, the only other woman in the Senate when Mikulski arrived, was elected to the Senate in her own right.

When the Senate was in session and Kassebaum needed to use the bathroom, she had to stand in line at the women's room used by the tourists. Mikulski immediately eyed a lounge that was set aside for the senators' wives. It was, she recalled in an interview, a memento of the days "when women would come over dressed in hats and gloves and sit adoringly listening to their husbands."

Once she explained her plight, the wives invited Mikulski and Kassebaum to use their lounge, which became their refuge until 1992. That was when four new women were elected to the Senate, making a grand total of six. The media announced "the Year of the Woman." It was a title Mikulski took with, um, a grain of salt: "Wow, we get our own year . . . like the Year of the Caribou, the Year of the Mushroom, the Year of the Asparagus."

They also got their own very modest two-stall bathroom. By 2013, there were twenty women in the Senate and waiting lines in the loo. Mikulski recalled that the Rules Committee, which controlled such matters, wanted to create an elegant place with a chandelier and little sinks with slim legs. "We wanted low cost. We didn't want anything fancy or expensive, but we wanted maximum functionality—the way women use a bathroom and not the way men think women use a bathroom," she recounted.

In the end, functionality won. The new bathroom had two more stalls, an extra sink, and shelves in which each senator had her own basket to store combs, brushes, makeup, whatever. "And so when I leave they'll retire my basket. . . . It's kind of like retiring your jersey," Mikulski said, rather proudly. In Washington, Mikulski has always exhibited a highly unusual combination of feistiness and bipartisanship. Susan Collins, Republican senator from Maine, recalled that when she first arrived, Mikulski immediately reached out.

"She didn't know me from Adam—or perhaps I should say from Eve," Collins said in a recent tribute on the Senate floor. "Yet, despite the difference in our seniority, our states, and our parties, she took me under her wing. . . . I was so grateful for her kindness and her wisdom. . . . She taught me the ropes of the appropriations process and instituted regular bipartisan dinners for the women of the Senate."

Those dinners have become famous—especially since the male side of the chamber has become more and more viciously partisan. In the beginning, they were held in a Senate room named after the late Strom Thurmond, an infamous pincher of ladies' bottoms.

"I know, the irony," Olympia Snowe, the former senator from Maine, once told me.

Next session, women will compose 19.5 percent of Congress. "We went from 104 to 104—down one in the House, up one in the Senate," reported Debbie Walsh, director of the Center for American Women and Politics at Rutgers. Obviously we could do better, but on the plus side, we're just a sliver away from passing Equatorial Guinea when it comes to gender diversity in the nation's legislature.

Recently Mikulski and Collins invited their female colleagues for coffee, to welcome the latest generation of newcomers. It was a final gesture of outreach as Mikulski moved on into Senate history. She deserves some kind of permanent memorial. Maybe they could put a plaque in that bathroom. Or better yet, they could rename the Strom Thurmond Room in her honor.

Part IV

Moving Forward

The Men Feminists Left Behind

Jill Filipovic

Jill Filipovic is a former columnist for The Guardian *and former senior political writer for Cosmopolitan.com. "The Men Feminists Left Behind" appeared in the* New York Times *on November 5, 2016.*

On November 8, Americans may elect our first female president. While many of us are exhilarated at the idea of this feminist victory, the toll we've paid for coming so close to that historic barrier has been the most graphically sexist election in living memory. What this campaign has shown us is that while feminism has transformed American culture, our politics, and the lives of women, men haven't evolved nearly as rapidly. Women changed. Too many men didn't. What happens next?

For all of American history, white men have been both the dominant group and the default one. It was mostly white men in charge, and it was white male experiences and norms against which all others found themselves contrasted and defined. When Hillary Clinton started at Yale Law School in 1969, there was only one woman in the United States Senate. It was legal for a man to rape his wife, but abortion was mostly outlawed. Mrs. Clinton graduated as one of just 27 women in a class of 235, after being explicitly told that if accepted into law school, she would take the rightful place of a man.

Decades-long movements championing women's rights have challenged that system, breaking down the legal and social barriers that blocked women from the workforce, questioning the cultural rules that so often kept women silent, and giving women more control over their bodies and, by extension, their futures. The same year Mrs. Clinton graduated from Yale, the Supreme Court held that American women had a legal right to abortion; that, coupled with expanded access to contraception, meant that women flooded into colleges and workplaces.

For women, feminism is both remarkably successful and a work in progress: we are in the workforce in record numbers, but rarely ascend to the highest ranks. Sexual violence is taken more seriously than ever, but women still experience it, usually from men they know, at astounding rates. Women are more visible in public life and create more of the media and art Americans consume, but we still make up just 19 percent of Congress and 33 percent of speaking roles in the one hundred top-grossing films.

Still, young women are soaring, in large part because we are coming of age in a kind of feminist sweet spot: still exhibiting many traditional feminine behaviors—being polite, cultivating meaningful connections, listening and communicating effectively—and finding that those same qualities work to our benefit in the classroom and workplace, opening up more opportunities for us to excel. And while we do find ourselves walking the tightrope between being perceived as a nice bimbo or a competent bitch, there are more ways to be a woman than ever before. It's no longer unusual to meet a female lawyer or engineer. No one bats an eye if we cut our hair short, wear pants, pay with a credit card in our own name, win on the soccer field, or buy our own home.

Men haven't gained nearly as much flexibility. The world has changed around them, but many have stayed stuck in the past. While women have steadily made their way into traditionally male domains, men have not crossed the other way. Men do more at home than they used to, but women still do much more—on an average day, 67 percent of men do some housework compared with 85 percent of women. Male identity remains tied up in dominance and earning potential, and when those things flag, it seems men either give up or get angry. This, perhaps more than anything else, explains the rise of Donald J. Trump: he promised struggling white men that they could have their identities back.

There is also the simple fact that Mr. Trump is running against a woman after eight years of our first black president. For many of the men used to seeing their own faces reflected in the halls of power, this trend away from white male authority has simply become intolerable. Today, racial animus is particularly pronounced among Trump supporters.

Mr. Trump offers dislocated white men convenient scapegoats—Mexicans, Muslims, trade policies, political correctness—and promises to return those men to their rightful place in society. With his string of model or actress wives, his beautiful pageant girls on competitive parade, and his vulgar displays of wealth, Mr. Trump embodies a fantasy of masculine power reclaimed. Mrs. Clinton, an unapologetically ambitious woman running to take the place of a trailblazing, successful black man, symbolizes all the ways in which America has moved on—and in her promises to help alienated men catch up is the implicit expectation that they too must change.

It's tempting to write off people who refuse to evolve, especially if their candidate loses the election. But the ugliness of the Trump campaign is evidence of how white men existing in their own shrinking universe can be a real threat. For women, greater educational achievements, a lifetime in the workforce, and delayed marriage and childbearing mean our lives are more expansive and outward-looking than ever before. Working-class white men, though, have seen many of their connections to society severed—unions decimated, jobs lost, families split apart or never formed at all—decreasing their social status and leaving them increasingly isolated. That many white men are struggling surely contributes to Mr. Trump's popularity, but the driving force of this election is not money—the median household income of Trump primary voters was about $72,000 a year, $16,000 more than the national median household income—it's power, and fury at watching it wane.

White men have always seen the world differently than women and minorities, but the norms and views of white male America are now being cast as marginal and, sometimes, delusional. This is a stunning shift.

The different ways in which men and women interpret the same information is evident in responses to Mr. Trump. As of early October, more than half of men believed that Mr. Trump respected women either "some" or "a lot." That poll was conducted after the Republican nominee was on record calling women pigs and dogs, commenting about his own daughter's sex appeal, and labeling a former Miss Universe, Alicia Machado, "Miss Eating Machine." At the same time, nearly two-thirds of women said that Mr. Trump didn't respect them. While more men now agree that Mr. Trump doesn't respect women after the vulgar *Access Hollywood* tape came to light, more than four in ten continue to say that Mr. Trump respects us. Which really makes you wonder what these men think respecting women looks like.

The men feminism left behind pose a threat to the country as a whole. They are armed with their own facts and heaps of resentment, and one electoral loss, even a big one, will not mean widespread defeat. Other Republican candidates are no doubt observing Mr. Trump's rabid fan base and seeing a winning strategy for smaller races in certain conservative, homogeneous locales.

In the last weeks of this ugly campaign, Mr. Trump has continued to talk about a rigged election and hint that he may not accept the results if he loses on Tuesday. While he is emboldening his followers to rage in the face of an electoral loss, Mrs. Clinton and her fellow Democrats are working to expand the ranks of women in elected office, giving the face of American power an even more extreme (and feminine) makeover. Democrats have been far better than Republicans at running diverse candidates, and if those candidates do well, the Senate could be almost a quarter female—a record high. Half of the candidates in the most competitive races to flip congressional seats from red to blue are women. Mrs. Clinton herself has reasserted her feminist identity, sometimes covertly: at both the Democratic National Convention and the final debate, she wore a crisp white suit, a sartorial homage to the white-clad suffragists whose victories are recent enough that a small number of women who were born before women could legally cast a ballot will be voting for Mrs. Clinton on Tuesday.

It's impossible to say whether a female president would help normalize female power and heal some of the rifts made visible by this election, or if she would enrage so many men that these gaps will only cleave wider. What is clear now is that this is the great unfinished business of the feminist project, a long-fermenting suspicion brought into bright light by this election: expanding roles and opportunities for women cannot usher in full gender equality unless men change.

Men don't need more masculine posturing or promises to restore them to forever-gone greatness. What they need is to make their own move toward gender equality, to break down the stereotypes and fetters of masculinity. Feminists, understandably, have focused on women; we have enough to do without being tasked with improving the lot of often-misogynistic men too. If the white men who feel ignored, disrespected, and lost want to see their lives improve, they should take a cue from the great feminist strides women have made and start to embrace that progress. Life really is better with more fluid gender roles that allow individuals to do what they're good at instead of what's socially prescribed. Every feminist I know will tell you that men bring much more to the table than physical strength or a paycheck, and that we would love a world in which men were free to be resilient and tender, ambitious and nurturing, expressive and emotional.

Donald Trump may not agree. But women make up half the country, and since we aren't going back in time, the same men who have long been hostile to feminism should consider coming along with us. I suspect for a lot of men, a more equal America—one with fewer cultural rules about how a man should be, and more avenues to identity and respect—would be a pretty great America to live in.

An Open Letter to White Liberal Feminists

LeRhonda Manigault-Bryant

LeRhonda Manigault-Bryant is associate professor of Africana studies and associate dean of the faculty at Williams College. "An Open Letter to White Liberal Feminists" appeared on the African American Intellectual History Society's website Black Perspectives *on November 19, 2016.*

Dear White Liberal Feminists,

After Donald J. Trump's election to the highest and most powerful political office of the United States last week, many of you have approached me, and my black brothers and sisters especially, with tearful eyes and somber faces. In person, in private, in public, and in the digital sphere, you have bemoaned the state of this world and our political landscape. You have lamented the deep-seated divisiveness of this country. You have wept, you have hugged, and you have gingerly asked, "How *are* you?"

And yet, your actions and inquiries are especially loaded, as much for their selfishness as their disingenuous nature. Your hugs and tears are of the self-soothing kind. Your inquiries seldom derive from a true desire to learn about how I, as an African American woman, *really* feel. Rather, your queries posit, in the most passive-aggressive way, "Aren't you as upset about the election results as I am?" "Aren't you embarrassed to be who you are?" "Aren't you sorrowful that your parents, and your in-laws, and your siblings, and your friends in towns and cities and states voted for Donald Trump?" "Aren't you ashamed to know that the women of your race also voted against so very many of their and others' interests?" "Aren't you devastated that the first female candidate—*our* candidate—to earn the presidential nomination for a major party did not win and allow *us* to make history for women?"

I am none of those things and I share none of these sentiments, in large part because these queries are not my narrative. I am ultimately not surprised by the most recent outcome of the election (and I am familiar enough with history to recall the inimitable Shirley Chisholm, the queen of the "unbossed and unbought" perspective). I find your overall shock at the role white women voters played in the election curious for its naïveté and annoying for its obtuseness.

If there is a sentiment we share, it is disappointment. I am disappointed that it has taken you this long to actually get what black women—and namely black feminists and womanists—have been trying to help you see and feel for a very long time. We now, for example, share fear. But my fear has been tempered by the legacy of slavery and antiblack racism in this country. You *now* worry for your children, your family, and your brothers and sisters. I *have been* worrying for mine.

And if I am being honest (and we can be honest, right?), I am also a bit delighted. I am delighted that you have received the potential awakening of a lifetime, and that now you might actually get what so many of us have been describing all along. Welcome to that deep perpetual angst. Embrace it, and allow it to motivate you to a deeper form of action.

I am also thrilled about how this moment might signal an end to the dangerous, disingenuous version of feminism that so many (though not all) of you embrace, and which promotes white women's success over and against anyone else's. It is the brand and tenor of white feminism that allows for a recapitulation of white male patriarchy (à la white women merely behaving as white men in drag and putting on the farce of gender equity). It has long been your trope and now it is your bane.

But what will you do with this newfound dismay? How will you interrogate and sustain your recent enlightened perspective about how white women remain complicit in the oppressions of so many nonwhite folks, and even themselves? Given your responses this week and the last, I am already seeing a kind of writing on the wall—that of denial. So few of you have commented on the implications of large numbers of white women voting against Hillary Clinton. So few self-proclaimed white liberal feminists interrogate racism, imperialism, capitalism, and sexism because they benefit from it and are too busy being protected by it.

What, then, is the efficacy of *this particular brand* of white feminism in our current moment? If this most recent presidential election has revealed nothing else, it has shown that this specific ilk of white feminism must die.

In this moment, if I have any regret, it is that you are trying to force me to be complicit in your self-denial and that you expect me to do yet another kind of labor. You look, of all places, to *me* to help you deal with your feelings. Rather than holding up your weeping, weak selves, I have a few questions for you to consider: *Who will you be in this hour? What will you do to enact change and with whom will you partner to do it?*

By all means, use whatever mechanism you require to move through the stages of grief as you bury your false idol of faux feminist solidarity. You must now do the intensive work to heal your troubled soul. And after you have come to terms with your own guilt, embarrassment, and pain, I encourage you to run with your newfound perspective. There is a terrifyingly beautiful lineage of black resilience—seasoned by black suffering—that you might turn to for hope.

I especially urge you to read up. A host of syllabi and materials posted on the African American Intellectual History Society website can help you, as can this powerful reminder from the Combahee River Collective's "A Black Feminist Statement":

> The most general statement of our politics at the present time would be that we are actively committed to struggling against racial, sexual, heterosexual, and class oppression and see as our particular task the development of integrated analysis and practice based upon the fact that the major systems of oppression are interlocking. The synthesis of these oppressions creates the conditions of our lives.

For more recent commentary, Kali Holloway's "Stop Asking Me to Empathize with the White Working Class: and a few other tips for white people in this moment" and a current call for a "Meeting in the Ladies Room" offer important perspectives, as does Yolanda Pierce's lament about the state of an already-fragile hope for racial and gender justice. Pay attention to brother Van Jones, who is truly out there doing God's work, and making a sustained, deep effort to get at what really divides us.

In the meantime, please stop assuming, listen attentively, and look deeply within yourselves to purge racism and sexism (and a whole litany of other 'isms). Most significantly, get yourselves together. And in so doing, remember that black bodies have historically been your solace in a myriad of ways. Embrace this opportunity to dismantle oppressions.

Ashes to ashes,
Dust to white liberal feminism.

Identity Issues Don't Distract from Economic Issues—They Are Economic Issues

Rebecca Traister

Rebecca Traister is a writer-at-large for New York *magazine and* The Cut, *and a contributing editor at* Elle *magazine. "Identity Issues Don't Distract from Economic Issues—They Are Economic Issues" appeared in* New York *magazine on December 11, 2016.*

The post-election period has seen an enormous amount of pushback against so-called identity politics—specifically the campaigns for social justice and representation for women and people of color—as a frustrating distraction from the serious economic concerns that affect a broad swath of Americans. If only we could get away from divisive "social issues," goes this line of thinking, Democrats could win elections and be able to enact progressive economic policies that would help far more people. But the idea that fights over reproductive freedom, sexual assault and harassment, LGBTQ rights, voting rights, criminal-justice reform, and gender and racial bias can be somehow separated from larger progressive economic stances is a fiction. As most people engaged in this argument know perfectly well, economic inequality is deeply wrapped up with gender and racial bias. The impending roll-back of social progress in a Trump administration will have a stagger-ing economic impact on this country's women, especially women of color, and regressive economic policies will take a disproportionate toll on those same populations.

It's worth remembering that two-thirds of all minimum-wage workers are women, along with 67 percent of all tipped workers—a fact that makes them vulnerable to sexual harassment by customers as well as employers. Women also dominate the home-health-care and child-care industries, in which wages are low, benefits anemic or nonexistent, and job insecurity, poor working conditions, and wage theft endemic. And women are especially reliant on government protections to keep them working safely and fairly.

"Start with the basics," says Heather Boushey, the chief economist at the Washington Center for Equitable Growth, who worked on Hillary Clinton's transition team. "Will there be enforcement of laws that make it illegal for business to discriminate against you, not hire you, or pay you less because you're a woman or a person of color or gay? It really comes down to the question: Is the government on your side? Is the government enforcing your basic rights as a worker?" That seems unlikely, given that the government will be led by a man who has said we should abolish the federal minimum wage, who has been sued by hundreds of former employees and contractors who claim he never paid them, and who has been accused of sexual assault by eighteen women.

Progressive economists point to Trump's appointments thus far as troubling evidence of just how bad the next four years could be for the lives and livelihoods of women and people of color. For secretary of labor we have Andrew Puzder, CEO of the company that manages the fast-food chains Carl's Jr. and Hardee's, which have been repeatedly investigated for wage theft; Puzder has also been a critic of minimum-wage hikes and the Obama administration's expansion of overtime-pay protection. For secretary of housing and urban development, we have Ben Carson, who criticized the Obama administration's push to bolster an element of the Fair Housing Act that addresses racial segregation and concentrated poverty as "mandated social-engineering schemes." Sarah Edelman, director of housing policy for the Center for American Progress, points out that "for a woman looking to buy or rent a home, the FHA is her greatest shield against a discriminatory landlord or mortgage lender." For attorney general, we have Senator

Jeff Sessions, a former prosecutor who aggressively pursued drug cases and has voiced his concern that drug prosecutions were down during the Obama administration. We know that African Americans are sent to prison for drug offenses at a rate six times greater than that of whites (even though black and white Americans use drugs at roughly the same rate), and a study published this month shows that "incarceration is negatively associated with ownership of a bank account, vehicle, and home among men and that these consequences for asset ownership extend to the romantic partners of these men."

Then there is the choice of Georgia representative Tom Price to head the Department of Health and Human Services. Price has a perfect record against reproductive rights. In 2005, he co-sponsored a bill that would define life as beginning at conception, which could have outlawed many forms of birth control. He also opposed the Affordable Care Act's coverage of birth control, claiming that there is not one woman who can't afford her own contraception. Price has company in his extreme stance in Vice President–elect Mike Pence, who as governor of Indiana introduced some of the most punishing antiabortion measures in the country and is the lawmaker who first floated the notion of stripping Planned Parenthood of federal dollars (which Republicans voted to do nine times in the last Congress alone).

The economic impact of dismantling women's health-care options cannot be overstated. In the first year that Obamacare covered contraceptive co-pays, women saved $1.4 billion on birth control alone. "If we reverse it," notes Planned Parenthood spokeswoman Erica Sackin, "that's a huge price tag women would now have to cover." But the ACA's advantages for women aren't just about contraception. "It's also a nondiscrimination measure so that women can't be charged more for health care," says Sackin. Before the ACA, it was legal for health-insurance companies to charge women more to exclude maternity care from health-care packages; meanwhile, in some states, insurance companies had been permitted to deny coverage to women who had been the victims of domestic violence or had had C-sections, since those could legally be considered preexisting conditions. All of those protections are now vulnerable; Price has voted to repeal Obamacare more than sixty times. This push to keep American women from accessing birth control and services that would permit them to exert control over their reproductive—and hence professional, personal, and economic—lives would be devastating, especially to economically vulnerable women.

What makes this all the more heartbreaking is that it stands in stark contrast to what could have been. After decades of work by progressives at the state and local levels, a spate of new federal protections and economic policies seemed, for a moment, possible with a Democratic Party that was leaning further left than perhaps ever before. On the Clinton campaign's agenda was a plan to mandate paid family leave and paid sick leave, to cap child-care costs at 10 percent of families' income, and to raise the wages of caregivers. Of course, a Republican Congress would have impeded the implementation of these ideas and reduced their scope, but now they will likely not even get an airing. Economists working on the Clinton economic agenda had hoped to redefine infrastructure spending to include a kind of human infrastructure as well. "We need bridges and tunnels, and we need our elders and children well cared for," Boushey explains. "These are both pieces of American infrastructure, and both create good jobs." It is also a notably gender-balanced approach. Trump has said that infrastructure will be a priority for him too, but a traditional infrastructure bill will create jobs in traditionally male-dominated fields. To do this while at the same time moving away from equal-pay protections and paid-leave policies that would help women is to once again make women far more dependent on male earnings than they have been in the recent past. As became clear in the campaign, to Trump, Making America Great Again means taking it back in time, to a period of draconian restrictions on reproductive autonomy, enormous economic inequality for women and minorities, and fewer protections for women and people of color in the workforce.

Political Correctness: How the Right Invented a Phantom Enemy

Moira Weigel

Moira Weigel's writing has appeared in The Guardian, The Nation, *the* New Republic, N+1, *and elsewhere. She is the author of* Labor of Love. *"Political Correctness: How the Right Invented a Phantom Enemy" appeared in* The Guardian *on November 30, 2016.*

Three weeks ago, around a quarter of the American population elected to the presidency a demagogue with no prior experience in public service. In the eyes of many of his supporters, this lack of preparation was not a liability, but a strength. Donald Trump had run as a candidate whose primary qualification was that he was not "a politician." Depicting yourself as a "maverick" or an "outsider" crusading against a corrupt Washington establishment is the oldest trick in American politics—but Trump took things further. He broke countless unspoken rules regarding what public figures can or cannot do and say.

Every demagogue needs an enemy. Trump's was the ruling elite, and his charge was that they were not only failing to solve the greatest problems facing Americans, they were trying to stop anyone from even talking about those problems. "The special interests, the arrogant media, and the political insiders, don't want me to talk about the crime that is happening in our country," Trump said in one late-September speech. "They want me to just go along with the same failed policies that have caused so much needless suffering."

Trump claimed that Barack Obama and Hillary Clinton were

willing to let ordinary Americans suffer because their first priority was political correctness. "They have put political correctness above common sense, above your safety, and above all else," Trump declared after a Muslim gunman killed forty-nine people at a gay nightclub in Orlando. "I refuse to be politically correct." What liberals might have seen as language changing to reflect an increasingly diverse society—in which citizens attempt to avoid giving needless offense to one another—Trump saw as a conspiracy.

Throughout an erratic campaign, Trump consistently blasted political correctness, blaming it for an extraordinary range of ills and using the phrase to deflect any and every criticism. During the first debate of the Republican primaries, Fox News host Megyn Kelly asked Trump how he would answer the charge that he was "part of the war on women."

"You've called women you don't like 'fat pigs,' 'dogs,' 'slobs,' and 'disgusting animals,'" Kelly pointed out. "You once told a contestant on *Celebrity Apprentice* it would be a pretty picture to see her on her knees . . ."

"I think the big problem this country has is being politically correct," Trump answered, to audience applause. "I've been challenged by so many people, I don't frankly have time for total political correctness. And to be honest with you, this country doesn't have time either."

Trump used the same defense when critics raised questions about his statements on immigration. In June 2015, after Trump referred to Mexicans as "rapists," NBC, the network that aired his reality show *The Apprentice*, announced that it was ending its relationship with him. Trump's team retorted that "NBC is weak, and like everybody else is trying to be politically correct."

In August 2016, after saying that the US district judge Gonzalo Curiel of San Diego was unfit to preside over the lawsuit against Trump University because he was Mexican American and therefore likely to be biased against him, Trump told CBS News that this was "common sense." He continued: "We have to stop being so politically correct in this country." During the second presidential debate, Trump answered a question about his proposed "ban on Muslims" by stating: "We could be very politically correct, but whether we like it or not, there is a problem."

Every time Trump said something "outrageous" commentators suggested he had finally crossed a line and that his campaign was now doomed. But time and again, Trump supporters made it clear that they liked him because he wasn't afraid to say what he thought. Fans praised the *way* Trump talked much more often than they mentioned his policy proposals. He tells it like it is, they said. He speaks his mind. He is not politically correct.

Trump and his followers never defined "political correctness," or specified who was enforcing it. They did not have to. The phrase conjured powerful forces determined to suppress inconvenient truths by policing language.

There is an obvious contradiction involved in complaining at length, to an audience of hundreds of millions of people, that you are being silenced. But this idea—that there is a set of powerful, unnamed actors who are trying to control everything you do, right down to the words you use—is trending globally right now. Britain's right-wing tabloids issue frequent denunciations of "political correctness gone mad" and rail against the smug hypocrisy of the "metropolitan elite." In Germany, conservative journalists and politicians are making similar complaints: after the assaults on women in Cologne last New Year's Eve, for instance, the chief of police Rainer Wendt said that leftists pressuring officers to be *politisch korrekt* had prevented them from doing their jobs. In France, Marine Le Pen of the Front National has condemned more traditional conservatives as "paralyzed by their fear of confronting political correctness."

Trump's incessant repetition of the phrase has led many writers since the election to argue that the secret to his victory was a backlash against excessive "political correctness." Some have argued that Hillary Clinton failed because she was too invested in that close relative of political correctness, "identity politics." But upon closer examination, "political correctness" becomes an impossibly slippery concept. The term is what ancient Greek rhetoricians would have called an "exonym": a term for another group, which signals that the speaker does not belong to it. Nobody ever describes themselves as "politically correct." The phrase is only ever an accusation.

If you say that something is *technically* correct, you are suggesting that it is wrong—the adverb before "correct" implies a "but." To say, however, that a statement is *politically* correct hints at something more insidious. Namely, that the speaker is acting in bad faith. He or she has ulterior motives, and is hiding the truth in order to advance an agenda or to signal moral superiority. To say that someone is being "politically correct" discredits them twice. First, they are wrong. Second, and more damningly, they know it.

If you go looking for the origins of the phrase, it becomes clear that there is no neat history of political correctness. There have only been campaigns *against* something called political correctness. For twenty-five years, invoking this vague and ever-shifting enemy has been a favorite tactic of the right. Opposition to political correctness has proved itself a highly effective form of crypto-politics. It transforms the political landscape by acting as if it is not political at all. Trump is the deftest practitioner of this strategy yet.

Most Americans had never heard the phrase "politically correct" before 1990, when a wave of stories began to appear in newspapers and magazines. One of the first and most influential was published in October 1990 by the *New York Times* reporter Richard Bernstein, who warned—under the headline "The Rising Hegemony of the Politically Correct"—that the country's universities were threatened by "a growing intolerance, a closing of debate, a pressure to conform."

Bernstein had recently returned from Berkeley, where he had been reporting on student activism. He wrote that there was an "unofficial ideology of the university," according to which "a cluster of opinions about race, ecology, feminism, culture and foreign policy defines a kind of 'correct' attitude toward the problems of the world." For instance, "Biodegradable garbage bags get the PC seal of approval. Exxon does not."

Bernstein's alarming dispatch in America's paper of record set off a chain reaction, as one mainstream publication after another rushed to denounce this new trend. The following month, the *Wall Street Journal* columnist Dorothy Rabinowitz decried the "brave new world of ideological zealotry" at American universities. In December, the cover of *Newsweek*—with a circulation of more than three million—featured the headline "Thought Police" and yet another ominous warning: "There's a 'politically correct' way to talk about race, sex and ideas. Is this the New Enlightenment—or the New McCarthyism?" A similar story graced the cover of *New York* magazine in January 1991—inside, the magazine proclaimed that "The New Fascists" were taking over universities. In April, *Time* magazine reported on "a new intolerance" that was on the rise across campuses nationwide.

If you search ProQuest, a digital database of US magazines and newspapers, you find that the phrase "politically correct" rarely appeared before 1990. That year, it turned up more than 700 times. In 1991, there are more than 2,500 instances. In 1992, it appeared more than 2,800 times. Like Indiana Jones movies, these pieces called up enemies from a mélange of old wars: they compared the "thought police" spreading terror on university campuses to fascists, Stalinists, McCarthyites, "Hitler Youth," Christian fundamentalists, Maoists, and Marxists.

Many of these articles recycled the same stories of campus controversies from a handful of elite universities, often exaggerated or stripped of context. The *New York* magazine cover story opened with an account of a Harvard history professor, Stephan Thernstrom, being attacked by overzealous students who felt he had been racially insensitive: "Whenever he walked through the campus that spring, down Harvard's brick paths, under the arched gates, past the fluttering elms, he found it hard not to imagine the pointing fingers, the whispers. Racist. There goes *the racist*. It was hellish, this persecution."

In an interview that appeared soon afterward in *The Nation*, Thernstrom said the harassment described in the *New York* article had never happened. There had been one editorial in the *Harvard Crimson* student newspaper criticizing his decision to read extensively from the diaries of plantation owners in his lectures. But the description of his harried state was pure "artistic license." No matter: the image of college students conducting witch hunts stuck. When Richard Bernstein published a book based on his *New York Times* reporting on political correctness, he called it *Dictatorship of Virtue: Multiculturalism and the Battle for America's Future*—a title alluding to the Jacobins of the French Revolution. In the book he compared American college campuses to France during the Reign of Terror, during which tens of thousands of people were executed within months.

None of the stories that introduced the menace of political correctness could pinpoint where or when it had begun. Nor were they very precise when they explained the origins of the phrase itself. Journalists frequently mentioned the Soviets—Bernstein observed that the phrase "smacks of Stalinist orthodoxy"—but there is no exact equivalent in Russian. (The closest would be *ideinost,* which translates as "ideological correctness." But that word has nothing to do with disadvantaged people or minorities.) The intellectual historian L. D. Burnett has found scattered examples of doctrines or people being described as "politically correct" in American communist publications from the 1930s—usually, she says, in a tone of mockery.

The phrase came into more widespread use in American leftist circles in the 1960s and 1970s—most likely as an ironic borrowing from Mao, who delivered a famous speech in 1957 that was translated into English with the title "On the Correct Handling of Contradictions Among the People."

Ruth Perry, a literature professor at MIT who was active in the feminist and civil rights movements, says that many radicals were reading the *Little Red Book* in the late 1960s and 1970s, and surmises that her friends may have picked up the adjective "correct" there. But they didn't use it in the way Mao did. "Politically correct" became a kind of in-joke among American leftists—something you called a fellow leftist when you thought he or she was being self-righteous. "The term was always used ironically," Perry says, "always calling attention to possible dogmatism."

In 1970, the African American author and activist Toni Cade Bambara, used the phrase in an essay about strains on gender relations within her community. No matter how "politically correct" her male friends thought they were being, she wrote, many of them were failing to recognize the plight of black women.

Until the late 1980s, "political correctness" was used exclusively within the left, and almost always ironically as a critique of excessive orthodoxy. In fact, some of the first people to organize against "political correctness" were a group of feminists who called themselves the Lesbian Sex Mafia. In 1982, they held a "Speakout on Politically Incorrect Sex" at a theater in New York's East Village—a rally against fellow feminists who had condemned pornography and BDSM. Over four hundred women attended, many of them wearing leather and collars, brandishing nipple clamps and dildos. The writer and activist

Mirtha Quintanales summed up the mood when she told the audience, "We need to have dialogues about S&M issues, not about what is 'politically correct, politically incorrect.'"

By the end of the 1980s, Jeff Chang, the journalist and hip-hop critic who has written extensively on race and social justice, recalls that the activists he knew then in the Bay Area used the phrase "in a jokey way—a way for one sectarian to dismiss another sectarian's line."

But soon enough, the term was rebranded by the right, who turned its meaning inside out. All of a sudden, instead of being a phrase that leftists used to check dogmatic tendencies within their movement, "political correctness" became a talking point for neoconservatives. They said that PC constituted a left-wing political program that was seizing control of American universities and cultural institutions—and they were determined to stop it.

The right had been waging a campaign against liberal academics for more than a decade. Starting in the mid-1970s, a handful of conservative donors had funded the creation of dozens of new think tanks and "training institutes" offering programs in everything from "leadership" to broadcast journalism to direct mail fund-raising. They had endowed fellowships for conservative graduate students, postdoctoral positions, and professorships at prestigious universities. Their stated goal was to challenge what they saw as the dominance of liberalism and attack left-leaning tendencies within the academy.

Starting in the late 1980s, this well-funded conservative movement entered the mainstream with a series of improbable best sellers that took aim at American higher education. The first, by the University of Chicago philosophy professor Allan Bloom, came out in 1987. For hundreds of pages, *The Closing of the American Mind* argued that colleges were embracing a shallow "cultural relativism" and abandoning long-established disciplines and standards in an attempt to appear liberal and to pander to their students. It sold more than 500,000 copies and inspired numerous imitations.

In April 1990, Roger Kimball, an editor at the conservative journal the *New Criterion*, published *Tenured Radicals: How Politics Has Corrupted Our Higher Education*. Like Bloom, Kimball argued that an "assault on the canon" was taking place and that a "politics of victimhood" had paralyzed universities. As evidence, he cited the existence of departments such as African American studies and women's studies. He scornfully quoted the titles of papers he had heard at academic conferences, such as "Jane Austen and the Masturbating Girl" or "The Lesbian Phallus: Does Heterosexuality Exist?"

In June 1991, the young Dinesh D'Souza followed Bloom and Kimball with *Illiberal Education: The Politics of Race and Sex on Campus*. Whereas Bloom had bemoaned the rise of relativism and Kimball had attacked what he called "liberal fascism," and what he considered frivolous lines of scholarly inquiry, D'Souza argued that admissions policies that took race into consideration were producing a "new segregation on campus" and "an attack on academic standards." *The Atlantic* printed a 12,000-word excerpt as its June cover story. To coincide with the release, *Forbes* ran another article by D'Souza with the title "Visigoths in Tweed."

These books did not emphasize the phrase "political correctness," and only D'Souza used the phrase directly. But all three came to be regularly cited in the flood of anti-PC articles that appeared in venues such as the *New York Times* and *Newsweek*. When they did, the authors were cited as neutral authorities. Countless articles uncritically repeated their arguments.

In some respects, these books and articles were responding to genuine changes taking place within academia. It is true that scholars had become increasingly skeptical about whether it was possible to talk about timeless, universal truths that lay beyond language and representation. European theorists who became influential in US humanities departments during the 1970s and 1980s argued that individual experience was shaped by systems of which the individual might not be aware—and particularly by language. Michel Foucault, for instance, argued that all knowledge expressed historically specific forms of power. Jacques Derrida, a frequent target of conservative critics, practiced what he called "deconstruction," rereading the classics of philosophy in order to show that even the most seemingly innocent and straightforward categories were riven with internal contradictions. The value of ideals such as "humanity" or "liberty" could not be taken for granted.

It was also true that many universities were creating new "studies departments," which interrogated the experiences, and emphasized the cultural contributions of groups that had previously been excluded from the academy and from the canon: queer people, people of color, and women. This was not so strange. These departments reflected new social realities. The demographics of college students were changing, because the demographics of the United States were changing. By 1990, only two-thirds of Americans under eighteen were white. In California, the freshman classes at many public universities were "majority minority," or more than 50 percent nonwhite. Changes to undergraduate curriculums reflected changes in the student population.

The responses that the conservative best sellers offered to the changes they described were disproportionate and often misleading. For instance, Bloom complained at length about the "militancy" of African American students at Cornell University, where he had taught in the 1960s. He never mentioned what students demanding the creation of African American studies were responding to: the biggest protest at Cornell took place in 1969 after a cross burning on campus, an open KKK threat. (An arsonist burned down the Africana Studies Center, founded in response to these protests, in 1970.)

More than any particular obfuscation or omission, the most misleading aspect of these books was the way they claimed that only their adversaries were "political." Bloom, Kimball, and D'Souza claimed that they wanted to "preserve the humanistic tradition," as if their academic foes were vandalizing a canon that had been enshrined since time immemorial. But canons and curriculums have always been in flux; even in white Anglo America there has never been any one stable tradition. *Moby-Dick* was dismissed as Herman Melville's worst book until the mid-1920s. Many universities had only begun offering literature courses in "living" languages a decade or so before that.

In truth, these crusaders against political correctness were every bit as political as their opponents. As Jane Mayer documents in her book *Dark Money: The Hidden History of the Billionaires Behind the Rise of the Radical Right*, Bloom and D'Souza were funded by networks of conservative donors—particularly the Koch, Olin, and Scaife families—who had spent the 1980s building programs that they hoped would create a new "counter-intelligentsia." (The *New Criterion*, where Kimball worked, was also funded by the Olin and Scaife foundations.) In his 1978 book *A Time for Truth*, William Simon, the president of the Olin Foundation, had called on conservatives to fund intellectuals who shared their views: "They must be given grants, grants, and more grants in exchange for books, books, and more books."

These skirmishes over syllabuses were part of a broader political program—and they became instrumental to forging a new alliance for conservative politics in America, between white working-class voters and small business owners, and politicians with corporate agendas that held very little benefit for those people.

By making fun of professors who spoke in language that most people considered incomprehensible ("The Lesbian Phallus"), wealthy Ivy League graduates could pose as anti-elite. By mocking courses on writers such as Alice Walker and Toni Morrison, they made a racial appeal to white people who felt as if they were losing their country. As the 1990s wore on, because multiculturalism was associated with globalization—the force that was taking away so many jobs traditionally held by white working-class people—attacking it allowed conservatives to displace responsibility for the hardship that many of their constituents were facing. It was not the slashing of social services, lowered taxes, union busting, or outsourcing that was the cause of their problems. It was those foreign "others."

PC was a useful invention for the Republican right because it helped the movement to drive a wedge between working-class people and the Democrats who claimed to speak for them. "Political correctness" became a term used to drum into the public imagination the idea that there was a deep divide between the "ordinary people" and the "liberal elite," who sought to control the speech and thoughts of regular folk. Opposition to political correctness also became a way to rebrand racism in ways that were politically acceptable in the post–civil rights era.

Soon, Republican politicians were echoing on the national stage the message that had been product-tested in the academy. In May 1991, President George H.W. Bush gave a commencement speech at the University of Michigan. In it, he identified political correctness as a major danger to America. "Ironically, on the 200th anniversary of our Bill of Rights, we find free speech under assault throughout the United States," Bush said. "The notion of political correctness has ignited controversy across the land . . ." he warned. "And in their own

Orwellian way, crusades that demand correct behavior crush diversity in the name of diversity."

After 2001, debates about political correctness faded from public view, replaced by arguments about Islam and terrorism. But in the final years of the Obama presidency, political correctness made a comeback. Or rather, anti–political correctness did.

As Black Lives Matter and movements against sexual violence gained strength, a spate of think pieces attacked the participants in these movements, criticizing and trivializing them by saying that they were obsessed with policing speech. Once again, the conversation initially focused on universities, but the buzzwords were new. Rather than "difference" and "multiculturalism," Americans in 2012 and 2013 started hearing about "trigger warnings," "safe spaces," "micro-aggressions," "privilege," and "cultural appropriation."

This time, students received more scorn than professors. If the first round of anti–political correctness evoked the specters of totalitarian regimes, the more recent revival has appealed to the commonplace that millennials are spoiled narcissists who want to prevent anyone from expressing opinions that they happen to find offensive.

In January 2015, the writer Jonathan Chait published one of the first new, high-profile anti-PC think pieces in *New York* magazine. "Not a Very PC Thing to Say" followed the blueprint provided by the anti-PC think pieces that the *New York Times, Newsweek,* and indeed *New York* magazine had published in the early 1990s. Like the *New York* article from 1991, it began with an anecdote set on campus that supposedly demonstrated that political correctness had run amok, and then extrapolated from this incident to a broad generalization. In 1991, John Taylor wrote: "The new fundamentalism has concocted a rationale for dismissing all dissent." In 2015, Jonathan Chait claimed that there were once again "angry mobs out to crush opposing ideas."

Chait warned that the dangers of PC had become greater than ever before. Political correctness was no longer confined to universities— now, he argued, it had taken over social media and thus "attained an influence over mainstream journalism and commentary beyond that of the old." (As evidence of the "hegemonic" influence enjoyed by un-named actors on the left, Chait cited two female journalists saying that they had been criticized by leftists on Twitter.)

Chait's article launched a spate of replies about campus and social media "cry bullies." On the cover of their September 2015 issue, *The Atlantic* published an article by Jonathan Haidt and Greg Lukianoff. The title—"The Coddling of the American Mind"—was a nod to the godfather of anti-PC, Allan Bloom. (Lukianoff is the head of the Foundation for Individual Rights in Education, another organization funded by the Olin and Scaife families.) "In the name of emotional well-being, college students are increasingly demanding protection from words and ideas they don't like," the article announced. It was shared over 500,000 times.

These pieces committed many of the same fallacies that their predecessors from the 1990s had. They cherry-picked anecdotes and caricatured the subjects of their criticism. They complained that other people were creating and enforcing speech codes, while at the same time attempting to enforce their own speech codes. Their writers designated themselves the arbiters of what conversations or political demands deserved to be taken seriously, and which did not. They contradicted themselves in the same way: their authors continually complained, in highly visible publications, that they were being silenced.

The climate of digital journalism and social media sharing enabled the anti–political correctness (and anti-anti-political correctness) stories to spread even further and faster than they had in the 1990s. Anti-PC and anti-anti-PC stories come cheap: because they concern identity, they are something that any writer can have a take on, based on his or her experiences, whether or not he or she has the time or resources to report. They are also perfect clickbait. They inspire outrage, or outrage at the outrage of others.

Meanwhile, a strange convergence was taking place. While Chait and his fellow liberals decried political correctness, Donald Trump and his followers were doing the same thing. Chait said that leftists were "perverting liberalism" and appointed himself the defender of a liberal center; Trump said that the liberal media had the system "rigged."

The anti-PC liberals were so focused on leftists on Twitter that for months they gravely underestimated the seriousness of the real threat to liberal discourse. It was not coming from women, people of color, or queer people organizing for their civil rights, on campus or elsewhere.

It was coming from @realdonaldtrump, neo-Nazis, and far-right websites such as Breitbart.

The original critics of PC were academics or shadow-academics, Ivy League graduates who went around in bow ties quoting Plato and Matthew Arnold. It is hard to imagine Trump quoting Plato or Matthew Arnold, much less carping about the titles of conference papers by literature academics. During his campaign, the network of donors who funded decades of anti-PC activity—the Kochs, the Olins, the Scaifes—shunned Trump, citing concerns about the populist promises he was making. Trump came from a different milieu: not Yale or the University of Chicago, but reality television. And he was picking different fights, targeting the media and political establishment, rather than academia.

As a candidate, Trump inaugurated a new phase of anti–political correctness. What was remarkable was just how many different ways Trump deployed this tactic to his advantage, both exploiting the tried-and-tested methods of the early 1990s and adding his own innovations.

First, by talking incessantly about political correctness, Trump established the myth that he had dishonest and powerful enemies who wanted to prevent him from taking on the difficult challenges facing the nation. By claiming that he was being silenced, he created a drama in which he could play the hero. The notion that Trump was both persecuted *and* heroic was crucial to his emotional appeal. It allowed people who were struggling economically or angry about the way society was changing to see themselves in him, battling against a rigged system that made them feel powerless and devalued. At the same time, Trump's swagger promised that they were strong and entitled to glory. They were great and would be great again.

Second, Trump did not simply criticize the idea of political correctness—he actually said and did the kind of outrageous things that PC culture supposedly prohibited. The first wave of conservative critics of political correctness claimed they were defending the status quo, but Trump's mission was to destroy it. In 1991, when George H.W. Bush warned that political correctness was a threat to free speech, he did not choose to exercise his free speech rights by publicly mocking a man with a disability or characterizing Mexican immigrants as rapists. Trump did. Having elevated the powers of PC to mythic status, the draft-dodging billionaire, son of a slumlord, taunted the parents of a fallen soldier and claimed that his cruelty and malice was, in fact, courage.

This willingness to be more outrageous than any previous candidate ensured nonstop media coverage, which in turn helped Trump attract supporters who agreed with what he was saying. We should not underestimate how many Trump supporters held views that were sexist, racist, xenophobic, and Islamophobic, and were thrilled to feel that he had given them permission to say so. It's an old trick: the powerful encourage the less powerful to vent their rage against those who might have been their allies, and to delude themselves into thinking that they have been liberated. It costs the powerful nothing; it pays frightful dividends.

Trump drew upon a classic element of anti–political correctness by implying that while his opponents were operating according to a political agenda, he simply wanted to do what was sensible. He made numerous controversial policy proposals: deporting millions of undocumented immigrants, banning Muslims from entering the US, introducing stop-and-frisk policies that have been ruled unconstitutional. But by responding to critics with the accusation that they were simply being politically correct, Trump attempted to place these proposals beyond the realm of politics altogether. Something political is something that reasonable people might disagree about. By using the adjective as a put-down, Trump pretended that he was acting on truths so obvious that they lay beyond dispute. "That's just common sense."

The most alarming part of this approach is what it implies about Trump's attitude to politics more broadly. His contempt for political correctness looks a lot like contempt for politics itself. He does not talk about diplomacy; he talks about "deals." Debate and disagreement are central to politics, yet Trump has made clear that he has no time for these distractions. To play the anti–political correctness card in response to a legitimate question about policy is to shut down discussion in much the same way that opponents of political correctness have long accused liberals and leftists of doing. It is a way of sidestepping debate by declaring that the topic is so trivial or so contrary to common sense that it is pointless to discuss it. The impulse is authoritarian. And by presenting himself as the champion of common sense, Trump gives himself permission to bypass politics altogether.

Now that he is president-elect, it is unclear whether Trump meant many of the things he said during his campaign. But, so far, he is fulfilling his pledge to fight political correctness. Last week, he told the *New York Times* that he was trying to build an administration filled with the "best people," though "not necessarily people that will be the most politically correct people, because that hasn't been working."

Trump has also continued to cry PC in response to criticism. When an interviewer from *Politico* asked a Trump transition team member why Trump was appointing so many lobbyists and political insiders, despite having pledged to "drain the swamp" of them, the source said that "one of the most refreshing parts of . . . the whole Trump style is that he does not care about political correctness." Apparently it would have been politically correct to hold him to his campaign promises.

As Trump prepares to enter the White House, many pundits have concluded that "political correctness" fueled the populist backlash sweeping Europe and the US. The leaders of that backlash may say so. But the truth is the opposite: those leaders understood the power that anti–political correctness has to rally a class of voters, largely white, who are disaffected with the status quo and resentful of shifting cultural and social norms. They were not reacting to the tyranny of political correctness, nor were they returning America to a previous phase of its history. They were not taking anything back. They were wielding anti–political correctness as a weapon, using it to forge a new political landscape and a frightening future.

The opponents of political correctness always said they were crusaders against authoritarianism. In fact, anti-PC has paved the way for the populist authoritarianism now spreading everywhere. Trump is anti–political correctness gone mad.

Part V

What Happens Next?

Feminism Lost. Now What?

Susan Chira

Susan Chira is assistant managing editor for news at the New York Times. *"Feminism Lost. Now What?" appeared in the* New York Times *on December 30, 2016.*

This was supposed to be the year of triumph for American women. A year that would cap an arc of progress: Seneca Falls, 1848. The Nineteenth Amendment, 1920. The first female American president, 2017. An inauguration that would usher in a triumvirate of women running major Western democracies. Little girls getting to see a woman in the White House. Instead, for those at the forefront of the women's movement, there is despair, division, and defiance. Hillary Clinton's loss was feminism's too.

A man whose behavior toward women is a throwback to pre-feminist days is now setting the tone for the country. The cabinet that Donald J. Trump has nominated includes men—and a few women—with public records hostile to a range of issues at the heart of the women's movement. A majority of white women voted for him, shattering myths of female solidarity and the belief that demeaning women would make a politician unelectable.

More broadly, there is a fear that women's issues as the movement has defined them—reproductive rights, women's health, workplace advancement, and the fight against sexual harassment, among others— could be trampled or ignored.

The Women's March on Washington on January 21 is an apt metaphor for the moment: movement as primal scream. It grew out of a post

on Facebook, was unconnected to any established women's organization, and has no set list of demands. Hundreds of thousands of women
say they are going, but will their anger turn into a broader movement?

"We need a 'come to Jesus' moment," said C. Nicole Mason of the
Center for Research and Policy in the Public Interest at the New York
Women's Foundation. "I feel like the denial is very severe." In the
weeks after the election, in conversations with nearly two dozen advocates for women, I heard the fractures of a movement still regrouping
after an unexpected defeat. They know that Mrs. Clinton didn't stand
for the feminist movement directly, and that you could vote against
her without saying you were voting against feminism. But one of the
movement's goals was shattering that ultimate glass ceiling. Some say
the failure to do so was so devastating that now is the time to rebuild
from the ground up. Others insist it's time to stay the course.

The challenges are a proxy for the questions the Democratic Party
must face over class, race, identity politics, and tactics. The women's
movement must balance how to broaden its message without losing its
base. Courting the white working class could alienate black women
still smarting over white women voting for a man many saw as racist—
a choice that seemed to put racial identity over gender solidarity. Some
younger women shun the feminist label altogether. It's not clear how
far the tent can stretch without leaving some outside.

The overall struggle is to stay relevant in the age of Trump. "Before
the election, even I was stunned by the sheer number of people I knew
who came forward saying they'd been survivors of sexual assault," said
Vivien Labaton, co–executive director of Make It Work, which promotes working families' economic security. "It's amazing to me the
lightning speed at which these issues have receded. The story is the total omission of women. Overnight."

Many veterans of the women's movement bristle at the thought that
the election was a rejection of feminism. Hillary Clinton won the popular vote by the largest recorded margin for a defeated candidate and
won the majority of all women's votes. Eleanor Smeal, president of the
Feminist Majority Foundation, cites a poll commissioned from Lake
Research Partners conducted on the eve of the election. It found that
59 percent of women voters overall, and 59 percent of younger women,
identify as feminists, up from 2012.

Heather Booth, long active in the movement, notes that polls consistently show majority support for childcare, equal pay, prohibitions against sexual discrimination, and the right to abortion. Ms. Smeal's and many other groups have reported intensified mobilization, donations, and volunteerism after the election. For many, the defeat may well be an awakening, a visible sign of barriers they thought had been swept away.

But this consensus masks real struggles.

Although exit polls suggest that a majority of young women voted for Mrs. Clinton, their enthusiasm for Bernie Sanders during the primary seemed to say that for some, feminism's traditional preoccupations seem out of date.

In late October, when the polls indicated that Mrs. Clinton would win, I sought out young women to talk about their perceptions of her. Jessica Salans, twenty-seven, who is running for local office in Los Angeles in 2017, said she found Mrs. Clinton's feminism outdated, failing to prioritize climate change, income inequality, and the toll of American intervention overseas.

"I saw a great documentary about the second-wave feminist movement, and it made me realize why people like Gloria Steinem were coming out in support of Hillary Clinton," she said. The brand of feminism that spoke to her, though, wasn't about breaking historic barriers. It was more specific: "progressive feminism, eco-feminism." To many inside and outside the feminist movement, the Clinton campaign message missed the mark.

"White working-class women saw Hillary Clinton as another privileged white woman wanting to break the glass ceiling," said Joan C. Williams, professor at the University of California, Hastings College of the Law. "That metaphor makes sense if your central goal is to gain access to jobs that privileged men have. Hillary's feminism was not about them."

Feminism, which at its heart should mean opportunities for women in every sphere, has also come to be seen as a proxy for liberalism, alienating conservatives.

S. E. Cupp, a columnist for the *Daily News* in New York and a conservative who did not vote for Mr. Trump, said: "There's a condescension that comes across from some in the women's movement. There's this idea that if you're not liberal, you're a traitor to your gender. Is our message alienating entire groups of people, including women?" She raised the provocative possibility that many women believed that Mr. Trump would keep the country safe in part because of his paternalistic, alpha male persona—and that was an implicit rejection of feminism's attempts to redefine gender roles.

Others worry that the women's movement has spent too much time policing language and behavior, blaming and shaming at the expense of dialogue. That, Professor Williams argues, can make misogyny attractive to the white working class, a way to rebel against condescending elites. The answer, some argue, is rebranding feminism—recasting issues in economic terms relevant to the working class, men as well as women.

"While the working families agenda is very strong, it's not big enough to get the country back on its feet," said Celinda Lake, a long-time Democratic pollster. "It needs to be embedded in a bigger economic message. Sometimes we talk about it in ways that make it sound like it's just for women, to the exclusion of men." By contrast, she said, Mr. Trump's economic platform was clear and compelling. Mrs. Clinton's calls for equal pay, childcare, paid family leave, and health insurance that covered birth control and mammograms paled before the appeal of someone who promised to bring back better-paying manufacturing jobs and restore a lost standard of living. The key is to link the two messages, to take issues that benefit women and show how they help families as a whole.

Ms. Lake described a focus group on equal pay she conducted with white union members in Michigan. She found that men were enthusiastic if they connected it with their own economic security. "One guy said, 'If the little lady doesn't get paid the same as I do, I need to get overtime and there's no OT anymore.'" The other men in the room, she said, agreed with him. Men may also be more receptive when the message is applied to their daughters. Reshma Saujani runs the group Girls Who Code, aimed at preparing girls for careers in technology. She noted that when her organization tried to persuade parents to enroll their girls, abstract appeals to gender equity fell flat. Evoking fathers' dreams for their daughters had more resonance.

"You've lost your home but your daughter has a shot at going back up to the middle class," she said, explaining why that kind of pitch succeeded. "We have to talk to different parts of the country differently. We can't make the same gender arguments—it doesn't work."

In these post-election conversations, the rawest wounds were those expressed by black women who felt betrayed by white women's support for Mr. Trump. These women worry that the national chest-beating about identity politics and the resolve to win back the white working class will come at their expense, subordinating issues of racial justice.

"You blame the people who voted for him, not the ones who didn't," said Salamishah Tillet, an associate professor of English and Africana studies at the University of Pennsylvania. Early organizers of the women's march faced scorn for initially failing to include minority women in leadership positions, then drew fire for the original name of the event—Million Woman March—which appropriated the name of a march by black women in 1997.

"Ashes to ashes, dust to white liberal feminism," wrote LeRhonda Manigault-Bryant, associate professor of Africana studies at Williams College, in an impassioned open letter noting that white feminists now shared the kind of fears long known to black women.

Rather than playing down race, these women argue it's essential to recognize its interconnection with feminism. Allowing racism to fester, they say, threatens not only black women but also white women, because it encourages white nationalism, which is also hostile to women's rights. But building bridges across racial and ethnic lines requires white feminists to understand that their experience is not universal, Professor Manigault-Bryant said. And it means defining women's issues as broadly as possible.

One of the paradoxes of 2016 was that some referendums on issues dear to the women's movement passed on the local level, from tax increases to expand child-care programs in Ohio to raising the minimum wage in four states. Advocates see opportunities in localities, a key battleground. The Michigan People's Campaign focused on a state house district called Downriver Detroit, dispatching campaigners door to door to talk across party lines about issues like caring for the elderly, disabled relatives, and children. Their progressive candidate won the local election, although Mr. Trump carried the same district.

Others see ballot initiatives as a potent weapon. "Maybe this moment was tailor-made for ballot measures as a critical form of policymaking and protest," said Justine Sarver, executive director of the Ballot Initiative Strategy Center. The center conducted polling in eleven states and found wide support for issues like equal pay, childcare, paid family leave, and higher wages and is gearing up for the 2018 midterm elections.

In the end, it's hard to argue that this election overall was a vote for the subordination of women. But it's a warning that feminism, as it has been defined, did not inspire enough people in enough places around the country. You didn't hear explicit calls for women to stay at home or be subservient to men, although it's an open question how many Americans are receptive to questioning traditional gender roles. Many who care about the place of women in American society are gripped by fears that men will now feel they have a free pass to demean women at home or in the workplace, that women's health, economic security, and reproductive rights will be dealt severe blows.

Talking to women who voted for Mr. Trump, I found many who were working, divorced or single, opinionated and outspoken. They saw Hillary Clinton as a menace and Donald Trump as an agent of change, if a flawed one. Many were living what might be called liberated lives. The challenge for the women's movement is to persuade more of the electorate that feminism is not merely a luxury for the privileged or the province only of liberals, but rather that it is essential to the freedom of every woman—and to her choices.

You Never Know What a Revolution Is Going to Look Like

Naomi Wolf

Naomi Wolf's eight bestselling books include The Beauty Myth *and* Vagina: A New Biography. *"You Never Know What a Revolution Is Going to Look Like" appeared in the* Sunday Times *on January 22, 2017.*

Never in twenty-eight years of feminist activism have I experienced standing in line at a bleak US highway rest stop, as a radicalized moment. But there I was—halfway between my home, New York City, and my destination, the Women's March on Washington—when things got surreal. I was buying fast food, and I noticed that women of all ages and backgrounds were wearing pink knitted hats with adorable cat ears. "What does the hat mean?" I asked. A woman who looked like a suburban Republican soccer mom said with a grin, "Pussy hats! It's the Pussyhat Project. For the march." And there, I noticed, was a hippie-ish sixty-year-old in a pussy hat, knitting another one, her daughter and young grandson nearby. There was a gaggle of college girls in pussy hats, defiant, tired, and laughing from the night on their overnight bus. Everywhere, the hats.

Later, in the ladies' room queue, I suddenly noticed an excited buzzing among usually silent, irritable women. Instead of the usual stoniness that comes with waiting for the women's restroom, while you can see men are zipping in and out of their own facilities nearby, there was an excited murmur among total strangers: "Are you going to the march? Are you going to the march?"

When I finally got to DC, there was almost no sign of the inauguration, except for blinking traffic signs showing road closings. But everywhere I looked—in the liquor store, on the metro—pink knit "pussy hats" on everyone. Women calling across crowded streets in staid Washington, DC Northwest, home of spies and diplomats, to pink-hatted absolute strangers: "Have a great march!" Then children, getting into the giddy mood of it, shouting at ladies in pink hats: "Have a great march!"

And I thought: you never know what a revolution is going to look like.

The Pussyhat Project is a clever grassroots movement: feminists who knit decided to create 1.7 million "pussy hats" to pass out at the March on Washington today. They added a note that goes with the hats, explaining women's issues and offering to connect to discuss them. This went viral in the United States. The mainstream talk show hosts at the hit show *The View* wore their "pussy hats" on camera. *USA Today* headlined the movement. Handmade pussy hats on Etsy had notes explaining that the product wouldn't arrive by the twenty-first—a sure sign of mainstream acceptance, both of the hats and of the march.

In twenty-eight years of feminist activism, I have never seen such a mainstream, grassroots, don't f— with the ladies March on Washington.

Usually, when I write about feminist activism, I write from the head: I could describe the way this march seemed to be taking fire as a backlash against what many on both sides of the aisle saw as the belittling, debasing treatment of women in the presidential campaign. I could describe the way progressive forces in America are mobilizing after the election of Trump, and how women's groups are anticipating a bloody struggle over gender issues that many had thought resolved for good in this century. I could critique the way the organizers of this march made mistakes. For instance, I certainly much regret their public, embarrassing retracted inclusion of pro-life feminists, following standard-issue criticism from standard-issue feminists. This retraction came, even as the organizers made claims for "diversity."

But I don't want to single out missteps. This march finally feels different; it feels like the maturation at last of a movement that has long been in adolescence. So it is more appropriate to write from the heart.

Today, in DC, as this historic march unfolds, it seems more accurate, even historically, to report not as a social critic or a feminist advocate, but as a feminist mom.

I joined up with my daughter Rosa at a meeting point on the march at eight in the morning. It had been at her invitation. I hadn't known for sure, when I was raising her, if her generation would find or, even better, make, any of their own meanings, in this movement. But she and her peers had ridden, like so many other young women, all night long on a chartered bus to get here.

She rode here with thirty of her classmates from her midwestern liberal arts college. It wasn't at the suggestion of any middle-aged feminists. It was these young women's own idea, arising from their own passion, their own sense of justice and inner need. This is their Freedom Summer.

Like groups of women across the country, they raised their own money. They lobbied the college alumnae for food funds—already a sign of organizational sophistication. They chartered their own bus— no depressive women's center in the basement for this generation. The organizer of the trip sent out to all participants careful prep points, including the website of the ACLU on one's rights to protest. My motherly instincts wanted to add the National Lawyers Guild phone number for if they got arrested. These young women arranged their own itinerary. Some young men are accompanying them, because these young women aren't as ideologically rigid as two generations back were (or, perhaps, had to be).

These young feminists are having fun with their strong, serious protestant voices. They are savvy about politics and making change. They are not scared to engage with power and to be in the face of the leader of the free world. They are beautiful. They are funny. They are badass. These are all of our daughters—even if we have no literal children of our own. I am so proud of them. And I am so proud, too, of my own generation.

This movement is more than alive. It is central, it is winning, it is making sense.

For twenty-eight years, I, like other women of my generation, have had to have stupid conversations. "Yes, rape is bad." "No means no." "Paying different wages for the same work is wrong." Over and over and over. And it seemed for decades, or day by day, as if we were condemned to be a shrieking irascible minority forever, and then die away, with the wind erasing the names on our headstones.

Instead—all that boring, infuriating, frustrating labor paid off. We moved the dial.

These young women grew up seeing women organize for their rights, whether they were minimum-wage workers or sex workers or nannies or miners or firefighters. They saw women name and bring lawsuits against their powerful, smug, institutionally protected harassers. They saw women lead nations. They saw women in the media fight and fight to get women covered seriously in the news, feature, and opinion pages. They even saw celebrities speak up against assault, against trafficking, against domestic violence. They saw men start to speak up: their dads, their brothers, their lovers.

What we did mattered. History is not going to be done with us, this time, so easily. They might not get rid of our ideas this time just because we shall pass away.

If you study the history of women's rights, what you see is this emergence—an angry young generation coming to feminist consciousness again and again. Then you see them get older and history erases their achievements, obliterates their names and ideas. Then two generations later, young women start to look around at their lives and think, "I don't know how to name what I am seeing."

That is how history has managed women's past revolutions, has diluted and contained them. This time it just may not work. This march was a huge blow right in the heart of patriarchy, because this time, all of these generations are still alive and well and successfully talking to one another. Will this be the end of the fight? Will there be no more missteps, mistakes? Of course not. Tomorrow night we go home, all won't have been fixed, and patriarchy will still suck.

But no one who was here will forget this day. And as someone who has heard interviewers say for twenty-eight years, "Isn't feminism really over?" I have this to say, on behalf of myself as one angry, very proud mom, in awe of these smart, irate, beautiful young women: Feminism? It's here to stay. You won't outlive it this time. This time—buddy, it will outlive you.

Thirteen Women Who Should Run in 2020

Amy Davidson

Amy Davidson is a staff writer at the New Yorker. *"Thirteen Women Who Should Run in 2020" appeared in the* New Yorker *on December 12, 2016.*

Here is a New Year's resolution for Democratic women in politics: be at least as brazen as Republican men are in deciding whether to run for president. It's not just that Donald Trump had no record of public service and a long list of what might be considered disqualifying attributes and actions. Ben Carson had no experience in elected office, and other candidates had very little. Marco Rubio was greeted as the future of the party when he decided to run just two-thirds of the way through his first term. That was only two years' more experience in the Senate than Ted Cruz, one of the final contenders, had. In 2017, there will be a dozen Democratic female senators with more experience. And why limit it to the Senate, or to any particular level of elective office? Women, in all professions, tend to feel they need to make their résumés perfect before putting themselves forward. Maybe they should stop thinking that way, at least in American politics, where insiderness does not seem to be particularly valued at the moment. Here's another test to think of before asking whether a woman is enough of a national figure to jump into the presidential race: How well known was state senator Barack Obama in 2004?

Hillary Clinton will not be the first woman president. But Americans are ready to elect one: despite the real misogyny that Clinton faced, this was a close election. And they should do it soon. (As Margaret Talbot notes, when it comes to women's issues, Ivanka is not the answer.) Here is a list of potential candidates to get started. But the premise—that there is room for a woman who isn't one of the very few that party leaders and commentators think of as "ready"—means that there are a lot of names missing from it.

1. **Amy Klobuchar**, senior senator from Minnesota. Popular, practical, appealing, progressive—picture her, for a moment, on a debate stage with Donald Trump, cheerfully taking him down. Why shouldn't she beat him? Klobuchar has been in the Senate since 2006. When a Minnesota television station asked her, just after the election, if she might consider running in 2020, she said, "We just got through a presidential race, and I love my job and what I do now, and more than ever we need people in the Senate that can work across the aisle." We might need people like Klobuchar in the White House even more.

2. **Elizabeth Warren**, senior senator from Massachusetts. She's already won some Twitter wars with Trump, whom she can rival as a communicator. And she knows something that a lot of Democrats, it seems, don't: where she wants the party to go. The drawback to a Warren candidacy is that it could lead Democrats to wallow in the what-ifs of 2016, when there was a push among progressives for her to run, rather than focus on the possibilities of 2020.

3. **Tulsi Gabbard**, US representative from Hawaii, combat veteran. She resigned from her position on the Democratic National Committee to endorse and campaign for Bernie Sanders, whose name she placed into nomination at the party's convention. (At thirty-five, she is less than half Sanders's age.) She would come into the race with the goodwill of his supporters. She is the first Hindu member of Congress, could she also be the first Hindu president? Maybe it's worth finding out; that's what primaries are for. She was one of the few people who came out of the Podesta e-mail hacking looking reasonably well, thanks to messages from Democratic donors about their clumsy attempts to punish her for backing Sanders.

4. **Kamala Harris**, attorney general and senator-elect from California. She is charismatic and deserves credit for some of Clinton's popular-vote margin, which was largely racked up in California, where people came out for the Senate race. As a state attorney general, she confronted financial institutions. That won't hurt in 2020.

5. **Claire McCaskill**, senior senator from Missouri. She has won election in a red state twice—in 2012, by beating Todd Akin in a race that gained national attention because of his outrageous comments about women, "legitimate rape," and abortion. One benefit of a McCaskill candidacy would be her willingness to mix it up. She has also been criticized for tweeting a bit too much and too adeptly—but is that a minus or a plus?

6. **Sheryl Sandberg**, Facebook's chief operating officer. Sandberg is ambitious and talented and a far better businessperson than Donald Trump. (She helped build Google; she could also help fund her own campaign.) And she also has some public-service experience—in the Treasury Department, where she worked with Lawrence Summers. She could lean in on the debate stage. Sandberg supported Clinton in the presidential election, and, when Democrats were assembling a Clinton cabinet of the mind, she was mentioned as a possibility for Commerce or the Treasury. Maybe it's time for her to start thinking about her own cabinet picks.

7. **Kirsten Gillibrand**, junior senator from New York. She is just a couple of steps behind Hillary Clinton, in terms of her relations with leading members of the party establishment. She is sometimes said to want the big job a little too much—but let's throw that thinking right out. An ambitious woman who sees a path forward for herself is a good, good thing. Gillibrand has also been exemplary in her efforts to get women to run at all levels of public office. Coming from New York, where there is some money to be found, won't hurt.

8. **Maggie Hassan**, governor and senator-elect from New Hampshire. She has the executive experience; this year, she won a tight, tough

race against Kelly Ayotte, and her victory and the turnout she inspired may have cost Trump New Hampshire. Maybe she can cost him the White House.

9. **Val Demings**, US representative-elect from Florida. "I carry a 9-mm. gun in my Dooncy & Bourke that was a gift when I retired from the police department," Demings told *Marie Claire*, in 2012, when she first ran for Congress. Demings, who had been the first female police chief of Orlando, didn't win that time, but she was back in 2016. An African American, she overcame the poverty and segregation of her childhood in Florida (a swing state, if anyone needed to be reminded). In every respect, she is a determined fighter and a compelling presence. Also, Demings's husband would be the first former sheriff to serve as First Spouse.

10. **Tammy Duckworth**, US representative and senator-elect from Illinois, combat veteran. Duckworth lost both her legs when the US Army helicopter she was flying was shot down over Iraq. She wouldn't be the first president to rely on a wheelchair, though she would be the first not obliged to keep it secret. Her debate against her Republican opponent, Senator Mark Kirk, gained some attention when he responded to her pride at being a member of the Daughters of the American Revolution with a crack about not knowing that her "parents came all the way from Thailand to serve George Washington." Her mother's family is Thai-Chinese; on her father's side, there is a record of military service that goes back to the earliest days of the nation. She could find new ways for her family to serve the country.

11. **Tammy Baldwin**, junior senator from Wisconsin. Another Tammy, and another woman who has found a way to win in a state that has recently favored Republicans. Baldwin has been credited with helping to make sure that the provision allowing young people to stay on their parents' insurance until the age of twenty-six was part of Obamacare; that measure has been so popular that Trump is claiming that he'll protect it. She voted against the Iraq War and is known, generally, as a strong progressive, and as one of those trying to find a new voice for the Democratic Party. An anxious assembler of traditional markers of

"electability" might note that she is openly lesbian. (She was the first openly LGBT person of either gender elected to the Senate.) Here's an answer to that: So what? Those are two words that women in politics should be saying a lot more often.

And, because President Trump could use a primary challenge, here are a couple of Republican women too:

12. **Susan Collins**, senior senator from Maine. Collins was one of the few Republican leaders who clearly stepped away from Trump during the campaign. She is also one of the few remaining moderates in the GOP. A run on her part might bring some focus to those Republicans who are thinking again about what their party has come to stand for.

13. **Nikki Haley**, governor of South Carolina, UN ambassador-to-be. Here's a potential plot twist: Haley, who was reasonably clear-eyed about Trump during the campaign, comes to her senses after working for him for a while, quits loudly, and runs against him. Getting foreign-policy experience to run for president in 2024 may be why she took Trump's offer. Maybe she should get that plan going sooner.

How a Fractious Women's Movement Came to Lead the Left

Amanda Hess

Amanda Hess is a staff writer for Slate *and a David Carr Fellow at the* New York Times. *"How a Fractious Women's Movement Came to Lead the Left" appeared in the* New York Times Magazine *on February 7, 2017.*

Hours before the start of the Women's March on Washington on January 21, every Metro car leading to the National Mall was packed so tight that it could take on no more riders. At station after station, the train doors would open, and the passengers would look out on throngs of fellow protesters—women, men, children, babies, the occasional dog—waiting on the platform. As people emerged from underground into the morning air, it was hard to tell where to go, so they found their way by gauging the human density, moving until they reached a spot so full of people that they could no longer move at all. There was an enormous rally happening somewhere in there—activists and celebrities speaking into microphones—but much of the crowd couldn't see or hear anything except rumbling waves of cheers. By the time they were meant to march, the crowd was so large that it already stretched across the entire route, from the rally site near the Capitol to the Ellipse near the White House.

The signs they carried spoke to any number of issues: immigration, abortion, race, the environment, inequality, the new president. "Refugees Welcome," "Keep Your Laws Out of My Vagina," "Black Lives

Matter," "Science Is Real," "Flint Needs Clean Water," "Nobody Likes You." The handmade pink "pussyhats" that many marchers wore—a reference to Donald Trump's caught-on-tape boasts about grabbing unsuspecting women by the genitals—had been sneered at in the days before the march. They were called corny, girlie, a waste of time. Seen from above, though, on thousands of marchers, their wave of color created a powerful image.

It was, somewhat unexpectedly, one of the largest mass demonstrations in American history. Millions of protesters—estimates range from three to five million—took to the streets of Washington, DC; Los Angeles, California; New York, New York; Palm Beach, Florida; Boise, Idaho; even Fargo, North Dakota. Sister demonstrations were held in Thailand, in Malawi, in Antarctica. The energy of almost every group alarmed or incensed by Trump's election seemed to have poured into a single demonstration. That it happened on the day after his inauguration was not surprising. What was striking was that all these people had come together under the auspices of a march for women.

Just two months earlier, the left did not appear to be a unified front. The polls had barely closed before the infighting began. Some blamed Hillary Clinton for ignoring Wisconsin, or the Democratic National Committee for boxing other candidates out of the primary field. Some blamed identity politics, which made working-class white voters "feel excluded," according to Professor Mark Lilla of Columbia. Others blamed white people, particularly the coastal ones who couldn't get their heartland relatives on their side.

But a crew of bummed-out, angry women was still aiming its ire at Trump. In the hours after his victory on November 8, Teresa Shook, a retired lawyer in Hawaii, posted to Facebook, suggesting a march on Washington. Some women on the East Coast had the same idea. At first, these suggestions were so impulsive that they seemed almost metaphorical. But within days, tens of thousands of women had pledged to join in. Over the course of two months, the idea became something far bigger than initially imagined. Eventually, an entire organizing team would have permits, T-shirts, fleets of buses, portable toilets, celebrity sponsors, and support from Gloria Steinem. Men meekly asked their female family members and Twitter followers: "Are we allowed to join?" By the middle of January, with the event shaping up to be *the* anti-Trump demonstration, *New York* magazine writer Jonathan Chait worried that "Women's March" was too niche an organizing principle—it was a "bad name," he tweeted, a divisive "brand."

The opposite turned out to be true: women led the resistance, and everyone followed. A march for women managed to crowd a broad opposition force onto its platform. In the weeks since the march, that energy has only spread. After Trump's executive order halting travel from seven Muslim-majority countries, the march's striking proof of concept—hit the streets, and a surprising number of others will join you—fueled more spontaneous actions in unexpected places: outside courthouses, Trump hotels, airport terminals, the offices of Senator Mitch McConnell. At each protest, you were likely to see a few pink cat ears poking out of the crowd, a reminder of the opposition's first gathering. It seems unlikely that any other kind of march would have turned out quite this way. In this moment, it happened that "women" was the one tent large enough to contain almost every major strain of protest against Trump.

Those who know their feminist history might see a paradox here. The women's movement has not always been a site for unity. It has been marked just as deeply by its fractures, failures, and tensions. But more than a century of internal turmoil has also forced the movement to reckon with its divisions. Now the question is whether it can bring even more Americans into the fold.

Clinton's loss on November 8 was a pivotal, identity-shifting moment in the course of the American women's movement. In an evening, the would-be first female president was shoved to the side by what a sizable chunk of the nation saw as that classic historical figure: the male chauvinist pig. In parts of the popular imagination, it wasn't just a loss for Clinton or for the Democratic Party. It was a repudiation of feminism itself.

But Clinton has always been a wary avatar of feminism. In 2008, she didn't run for president as a "women's candidate"; if anything, she campaigned with her sex in the closet and the strategist Mark Penn advising her to harden her image into an American Iron Lady. "They do not want someone who would be the first mama," he wrote in one memo. Years later, HBO's *Veep* would satirize that posture through its own fictional politician. "I can't identify myself as a woman!" she tells

her staff. "People can't know that. Men hate that. And women who
hate women hate that, which I believe is most women."

In the eight years between Clinton's first and second presidential
campaigns, though, something shifted: feminism became fashion-
able. By the start of the Obama era, incisive women's blogs like *Jezebel*
and *Feministing* had already hit the web and started throwing pop-
corn at the big screen of American culture, covering the same topics
that women's magazines did—fashion, movies, sex—but taking on the
women's magazines too. By Obama's second term, this model had
thrived and multiplied so many times over that even a co-founder of
the sports website *Bleacher Report* started his own women's site, *Bustle*.
Soon enough, no corner of culture was safe from a feminist critique,
from Christmas songs to "manspreading." Pop stars—people like Lady
Gaga, Katy Perry, and Taylor Swift—were asked if they were feminists,
and if they shied away from the label, outrage would greet them online.

Feminism became increasingly popular, but in a very specific
way—one attuned to the concerns of people with office jobs and time
to spend online. The feminist priorities of this new media landscape
tended to involve topics that middle-class women would experience
firsthand: reproductive rights, catcalling, campus rape, professional
opportunity, pop-culture representation. The writers setting its tone
tended to be young women who were asked to produce large amounts
of clickable copy, for not much money, in very little time, exploring
feminist issues not through time-intensive reporting but through
"takes" on the women already making news: the work-life balance of
Yahoo's chief executive, Marissa Mayer; the pay gap between Jennifer
Lawrence and her male co-stars. Some content chased sexist slights
down to the most passing personal concerns, like an item from the
Huffington Post that sighed: "There is no proper way for a woman to
cut her hair, let alone do anything right in this world."

It's not that women's activist groups vanished or political organizing
stalled. But it did become possible for an American woman to cultivate
a relationship to feminism that was primarily consumerist: there were
feminist TV shows to watch, feminist celebrities to follow, feminist
clothes to buy. Unlike many other major social movements, women's
liberation dovetails neatly with an important advertising demographic,
a lesson capitalism absorbed more than a century ago. In 1908, the

advertiser J. Walter Thompson hired suffragists to address the growing women's market. Over the next decades, the industry would slip
women's rights messaging into ad copy. Old Dutch Cleanser offered
"freedom from household drudgery"; Shredded Wheat promised a
"declaration of independence" from cooking. These days, even our
bath products have achieved empowerment. Ads for Secret deodorant
nudge us to ask for a raise, and those for Always prompt us to challenge
stereotypes about girls. Dove wants us to feel beautiful at any size.

It's telling which strand of feminism these brands have deemed
marketable: the one that doubles as self-help. This is a vision of feminism in which the primary thing that needs to change is a woman's
frame of mind. Something similar happened to the pop stars who once
hesitated to call themselves feminists—they came around to feminism
by redefining feminism around themselves. To Lady Gaga, feminism
was about protecting "the integrity of women who are ambitious."
Taylor Swift realized, she said, that she had "been taking a feminist
stance without actually saying so." Feminism was being defined down
to its most benign interpretation. It was less a political platform than
a brand identity.

In 2013, *Lean In*, by Sheryl Sandberg, raised this pop-cultural sub-
text to the level of text. Sandberg called the book "sort of a feminist
manifesto," but it preached individual solutions to systemic problems,
encouraging women to focus on "internal obstacles" and "dismantle
the hurdles in ourselves." This feminist mode, where personal success
becomes synonymous with social progress, can be plugged into any
number of political orientations. The latest model for the corporate-
celebrity feminist brand is Ivanka Trump, who has built a lifestyle
company under the hashtag #WomenWhoWork. A recent pitch neatly
weds activist language with shoppable solutions: "We're committed to
solving problems. If we can't find a solution, we'll make it ourselves
(case in point: the Soho Tote, the ultimate work bag)."

By the time the 2016 campaign rolled around, Clinton wasn't just
permitted to run as a feminist—she was practically obligated to. Her
messaging shifted accordingly. Years of women debating the right way
to be a feminist had the side effect of forcing the first female major-
party candidate to the left. In 2008, she argued that she wanted abortion to be "safe, legal, and rare—and by rare I mean rare." In last year's

debates, she stopped qualifying her support. "I will defend Planned Parenthood," she said in one. "I will defend *Roe v. Wade*, and I will defend women's rights to make their own health care decisions."

Meanwhile, her campaign mimicked the aesthetics of the pop-cultural feminist mode. The candidate affirmed her feminism in a video interview with Lena Dunham, posed in a Kim Kardashian selfie, and made a cameo on *Broad City*. Her campaign posted a *BuzzFeed*-style listicle informing Latinos that Clinton was "just like your *abuela*." (With the Twitter hashtag #NotMyAbuela, those voters begged to differ.) Her site sold embroidered pillows that said "A Woman's Place Is in the White House" and a T-shirt with a big "Yaaas, Hillary!" printed over her senior portrait from high school. After Trump accused her of playing "the woman's card," her campaign introduced a free hot-pink "Official Hillary for America Woman Card" that drove more than $2 million in donations within days. One young woman earnestly prodded her at an Iowa campaign event: "If you could choose, would you rather be the president or Beyoncé?"

Pop feminism, having been washed of its political urgency, was now being integrated back into politics at the highest level. The candidate who once shrank from feminism was positioning herself as an icon of the movement. Her image became closely aligned with two metaphors—the pantsuit and the glass ceiling—that speak to a particular kind of woman: a corporate careerist at the top of her field. A "secret" Facebook group, Pantsuit Nation, popped up to encourage Clinton supporters to wear pantsuits to the polls. When she clinched the Democratic nomination for president last June—the one she would formally accept the following month, dressed in suffragist white—Clinton called back to the Seneca Falls convention of 1848, where "a small but determined group of women, and men, came together with the idea that women deserved equal rights." The feminist project started there, she implied—and she was going to finish it.

When Clinton lost, pop feminism suffered a crisis. As everyone pored over exit polls, some of the long-simmering fractures between different groups of women exploded into view. Ninety-four percent of black women voted for Clinton, but 53 percent of white women voted for Trump, perhaps more likely to see themselves in his vision of the world than in the pop feminism that fed Clinton's campaign. Despite

Trump's palpable, eminently bloggable disrespect for women—and that infamous tape—he had successfully courted a faction of female voters. His win suggested that Americans were more comfortable with misogyny than many had thought, but it also burst the bubble of cheery pop feminism, which had achieved its huge popularity at the expense of class consciousness and racial solidarity.

In some places, you could watch the mood turn in a matter of days. The Pantsuit Nation Facebook group ceased its celebrations and became a site for sharing stories of pain and resilience. But when the group's founder, a Maine educator named Libby Chamberlain, announced a plan to channel the power of the group in real life, it wasn't exactly a call to activism—it was a coffee-table book. "You are a force, Pantsuit Nation," she wrote. "Let's see if we can harness that force within the pages of a book and see it on night stands and coffee tables all around the world." The idea brought on a revolt. "The N.R.A. with its five million members has a stranglehold on Congress," one commenter wrote. "Pantsuit Nation has four million members and decides its main mission is 'storytelling' and now, selling books. What a colossal waste."

But for some outside observers, this was a productive comeuppance. LeRhonda Manigault-Bryant, an associate professor of Africana studies at Williams College in Massachusetts, published "An Open Letter to White Liberal Feminists," on the website *Black Perspectives*, expressing her disappointment that it had taken Donald Trump to shake them into her reality. "I am delighted that you have received the potential awakening of a lifetime, and that now you might actually get what so many of us have been describing all along," she wrote. "Welcome to that deep perpetual angst. Embrace it, and allow it to motivate you to a deeper form of action."

In those same November weeks, the nascent march-on-Washington project was navigating its own identity crisis. Some of the early organizers had romantic-comedy-type jobs—pastry chef, yoga instructor. One of the women, Bob Bland, a fashion designer, had amassed a small online following by designing "Nasty Woman" and "Bad Hombre" T-shirts and selling them online. "I had this whole network of 'nasty women' and 'bad hombres,'" she told me. "After the election, they were looking to me like, 'What are we going to do next?'"

Disparate organizers convened around a Facebook event announcing a Million Women March. There was one major problem with this: in 1997, activists organized a Million Woman March in Philadelphia to address the particular concerns of black women. When this new march on Washington unwittingly chose a very similar name, it crystallized the idea that the nascent movement was being run by a handful of white women with no organizing history. Comments began pouring in from all sides.

The organizers had stumbled into a conflict that has dogged women's organizing from the very beginning: of all the tensions that have coursed through the women's movement, none has ever been quite so pronounced as the one between white and black women. Consider what happened when Sojourner Truth showed up at a women's rights convention in Ohio in 1851. Frances Gage, the woman running the show, recalled the scene twelve years later: "The leaders of the movement trembled on seeing a tall, gaunt black woman in a gray dress and white turban, surmounted with an uncouth sunbonnet, march deliberately into the church, walk with the air of a queen up the aisle and take her seat upon the pulpit steps." A "buzz of disapprobation" spread through the church. White women in attendance complained that a black woman's testimony would distract from the convention's focus. "Don't let her speak, Mrs. Gage—it will ruin us," one said. "Every newspaper in the land will have our cause mixed up with abolition and niggers, and we shall be utterly denounced."

Throughout the convention, men arrived to speak out against women's suffrage. Women, they said, were too weak and helpless to be trusted with the power of the vote. Because "there were very few women in those days who dared to 'speak in meeting,'" as Gage put it, their points went unchallenged until Truth stepped forward. White women hissed, but Truth's very identity nullified the arguments coming from both men and women in attendance. "That man over there says that women need to be helped into carriages, and lifted over ditches, and to have the best place everywhere," she said. "Nobody ever helps me into carriages, or over mud puddles, or gives me any best place. And ain't I a woman? Look at me! Look at my arm!" She rolled up her sleeve to the shoulder. "I have plowed and planted, and gathered into barns, and no man could head me. And ain't I a woman?"

In that moment, Truth shattered an idea of white femininity that had been used to both underpin and undermine the cause of suffrage. As a slave, she had worked in the fields like a man; as a free black woman, she could not rely on the offerings of white male gentility. Gage wrote that Truth's testimony compelled the white women in attendance to embrace her "with streaming eyes, and hearts beating with gratitude."

But two years later, Truth still drew jeers from white crowds when she attended women's meetings. A vision of whiteness was ingrained in the leaders and the arguments of the mainstream movement. Even the suffragists' signature white clothes were deliberately chosen to signal purity. This ideal of feminine virtue did not extend to black women, or working-class ones. Some suffragists made their racism and classism explicit. In 1894, a white woman at a meeting of the Brooklyn Woman Suffrage Association complained that New York had become an "asylum for the trash of all nations," arguing that women's suffrage ought to be restricted. "Think what it means to give it to all women," she said. "Our criminal and pauper men have wives; there are thousands of female operatives in tobacco factories and similar fields of labor; there are probably two million Negro women in this country who are but little uplifted above the plane of animals."

One curious point of this history is that so many suffragists came from the antislavery movement. Elizabeth Cady Stanton and Susan B. Anthony, whose partnership would come to define the suffrage movement in the United States, started their activist careers as abolitionists. But after the Civil War, as black men and all women agitated for the right to vote, a political battle broke out over who would be enfranchised first. (Either way, black women would be last.) In 1865, Stanton lamented having to "stand aside to see 'Sambo' walk into the kingdom first," as she put it in the *National Anti-Slavery Standard*.

Over time, these racial contours would harden into lasting institutions. When women's social clubs spread across the United States at the turn of the century, two models emerged. Whites-only clubs leveraged middle-class women's leisure time to campaign for social reforms. Black women, who largely worked outside the home, came together around urgent needs. One of the first actions of the black Chicago Women's Club was to raise money to prosecute a police officer who killed a black man. The main distinction between clubs, the black activist Fannie Barrier Williams wrote, was that for black women, "it is not a fad."

Black women distinguished themselves not only as suffragists but also as vocal critics of a movement that pushed one kind of justice aside in pursuit of another. In 1913, when thousands of suffragists marched on Washington to agitate for the vote, black women were instructed to march in the back. Ida B. Wells defied the order and marched with the delegation from Illinois, her home state. She wasn't just protesting for her right to vote. She was protesting the protest too.

This dynamic is not only a thing of distant history: in the thick of feminism's second wave, women were often still divided along lines of identity. In 1967, as the best-selling author Betty Friedan called to order the first meeting of the New York chapter of the National Organization for Women, she found herself at odds with a black activist and lawyer named Flo Kennedy, who pushed the women around her to make common cause with the antiwar and Black Power movements. Friedan and the meeting's host—Muriel Fox, the highest-ranking female executive at the world's largest public-relations agency—were not pleased. As Kennedy put it in her memoirs, they "went bonkers."

Friedan's 1963 book *The Feminine Mystique* had been an awakening for a class of white, married, middle-class women, and she pictured herself as the leader of what she called a "mainstream" feminist movement. When women at one 1970 march offered her a lavender armband to wear in solidarity with a NOW member recently attacked for her bisexuality, Friedan dropped it on the ground, furious at the attempt to add gay rights to her program.

Kennedy continually pushed in the opposite direction, trying to build bridges between feminist groups and other movements. At one point, Friedan admonished her to leave the feminist movement alone and "focus her attention on matters of Black Power." As the second wave matured, black women found themselves continually calling on it to consider a new approach, one that acknowledged the different needs of different women. As the black feminist and leftist Barbara Smith told the National Women's Studies Association in 1979, any feminism that didn't account for the specific concerns of black women, poor women, disabled women, lesbians, and others was not really feminism—it was "merely female self-aggrandizement."

There has never been one women's movement. It's difficult, for example, to say that the American feminist project started in Seneca Falls, New York, in 1848, because black women were not invited to that convention. It's hard to say that electing a woman as president would have been feminism's crowning achievement, because the success of one woman does not naturally trickle down to all. The history of the women's movement is one of warring factions and sharp self-criticism. But its 150 years of navigating internal disputes put it in a position to lead what seemed, at the end of last fall, like a highly divided left.

"It's embarrassing to me now to say it, but I didn't know the term 'intersectionality' when we started," Bob Bland, the Women's March co-chairwoman, told me. Now she deployed it often to emphasize the growing diversity of the march. She told various reporters that she had met women working "in so many different intersectionalities" and hoped to reach a "wide intersectionality of people" in a march that reflected "all of the different intersections of human rights."

That magic word comes from a 1989 paper by the legal scholar Kimberlé Crenshaw that was published in the *University of Chicago Legal Forum*. Crenshaw had studied cases in which black women sued their employers for what appeared to be "compound discrimination"— both racial and gender biases. But they were often told they lacked legal standing: laws protected them from discrimination as African Americans or as women, but not specifically as black women. Crenshaw used a traffic metaphor to describe the interlocking forms of oppression a person might face. Cars flowed through an intersection in all directions; when an accident happened, it could have been caused by cars from any number of sides, or even all sides.

That metaphor would be plucked from Crenshaw's paper and grow in resonance over the next two decades, until "intersectionality" became a rallying cry—the main point of rhetorical resistance against the tide of single-issue feminist conversation. Even beneath the shiny surface of Obama-era pop feminism, dissenters took countless shots at its racial cluelessness, its lack of class consciousness, its sometimes shallow concerns. Women of color convened on Twitter under hashtags like #SolidarityIsForWhiteWomen to detail their experiences of being sidelined in feminist conversations, and many on the left criticized the way a trickle-down, professional-oriented feminism was becoming popular just as income inequality between women was ballooning. (It's hard to "lean in" to a job cleaning hotel rooms.) In recent years, intersectionality even popped up on People.com, on *Bustle,* and in a tweet from Clinton.

Often the criticism that lies behind this word is brushed off, met with defensiveness, taken personally. (As the founder of Pantsuit Nation wrote to critics of her book deal: "This is not the place for divisiveness.") Women turn to feminism because they want to stand up and say something; it can be jarring for them to be told to sit down and listen to someone else. But the concept became a useful tool for the march on Washington, which set about the task of uniting feminism's mainstream, popular arm and its dissenting factions—all in the space of two months.

Soon after the suggestion to march raced across the web, Vanessa Wruble—a white producer and co-founder of the media company OkayAfrica—made a pivotal intervention in its planning. "I thought the stakes were so high," she told me. "It needed to be an inclusive movement, or it was going to be a total disaster. I felt that it could damage the country." At this critical moment, with the march quickly ballooning into something bigger than the initial organizers could handle on their own, Wruble reached out and urged them to drop the name Million Women March. Then she linked them up with her network, and soon three seasoned activists—Carmen Perez, Linda Sarsour, and Tamika Mallory—got on board. These women hadn't necessarily supported Clinton, and they didn't necessarily identify as feminists. But they had experience organizing in communities of color and saw the march as an opportunity to reach a large new audience. When Sarsour got the call, she had just posted a comment on the march's Facebook page: "Can you include Muslim women and Muslim communities in the list?"

The three women—one Chicana Latina, one Palestinian American, one black—met through their involvement in Justice League NYC, a juvenile-justice initiative. In 2015, they organized a nine-day march from New York to Washington, ending in a rally at the Capitol that drew a small crowd. Now hundreds of thousands of women whose previous interest in justice may have been abstract at best were turning to them for leadership. The question, Perez told me, was "How do we get them to understand that their liberation is bound with ours?"

Meanwhile, the three had some catching up to do with the mainstream feminist perspective. "I don't have a lot of what I would consider to be deep, transformative relationships with white women," Sarsour told me. "I've been learning a lot," she said, and working toward becoming "more comfortable around this movement of feminism that I always felt didn't particularly include Muslim women." The organizers appeared on the hip-hop radio morning show *The Breakfast Club* and loaded their Instagram page with black feminist heroes. But they also posed for windswept photos in *Vogue*, and some dropped by the Wing, a private Manhattan women's club with a $2,250 annual membership fee. Their rally put Angela Davis on the same stage as Scarlett Johansson.

When I called Kimberlé Crenshaw in January, she had just returned home to Los Angeles from the march on Washington, where she walked with a group of women from the African American Policy Forum. Her group was so far back in the crowd that they couldn't hear the rally, and "I'm kind of glad about it," she told me. "We were in this sea of humanity." Wading through the crowd, she said, "I saw all the different issues and people that had found their way under the banner of the Women's March. It was the embodiment of the intersectional sensibilities that a lot of us have been working on for a very long time."

The women's movement's tendency toward a singular perspective is "not an exceptional problem for feminism," Crenshaw told me. "Patriarchy works in such a way that these critiques never even surface in a lot of movements led by men. This conversation isn't always happening in other spaces. And if the conversation leads to more robust ways of thinking about women, feminism, and social justice, it can be a very good thing.

"The million-dollar question is: Can these feminisms live together under an anti-Trump banner?" Crenshaw said. "It happened for twenty-four hours all across the world."

When I made my way back to my hotel after the march, the cheers of the crowd fading into the distance, I opened my laptop and saw a different version of what I had just seen in person. Now it was all filtered through my own social-media bubble—that of a middle-class white woman who lives in Brooklyn. Facebook's trending topics, tailored to fulfill each user's particular online habits, served me up a pop-celebrity version of the day's events. It pointed me toward the speeches of Scarlett Johansson and Madonna, and nobody else. As scenes of the march traveled through the media and across the web, the story spun out in even more directions. Twitter lit up with notes of internal dissent and snapshots of signs from the march: "Don't forget: White women voted for Trump" and "Black women tried to save y'all" and "I'll see you nice white ladies at the next #blacklivesmatter march, right?"

But for the moment, at least, Trump appears to be the great uniter. In the days and weeks since the march, its energy spilled into spontaneous actions across the country, with protesters coming together on behalf of Muslims and immigrants. Donations poured into Planned Parenthood and the American Civil Liberties Union. Congressional switchboards were inundated with calls. When the *Washington Post* polled Americans post-march, it registered a huge shift in energy among Democrats, especially Democratic women, 40 percent of whom said they planned to get more involved in activism.

But liberals are not the only ones drawing inspiration from the protests. Flip to Fox News, click around conservative blogs, or browse pro-Trump Twitter and you can watch the demonstrations fuel a different kind of opposition narrative. After the march, Fox News set clips of rally speeches to foreboding music. Breitbart published photos with the headline "See what a massive, Hillary-shaped bullet America just dodged?" The right-wing Media Research Center aggregated the most "vile and ridiculous signs." Twitter exploded with anti-Muslim attacks on Linda Sarsour, who was called a "terrorist" who "loves ISIS." When the annual March for Life hit the Mall to demonstrate against abortion rights, *The Blaze* called it "the real women's march." (The Women's March did, at one point, remove the name of an antiabortion group from its list of partners, after an uproar.) According to Public Policy Polling, 48 percent of Trump voters think the protesters who convened at airports to protest the travel ban were paid by George Soros. Trump tweeted recently: "Professional anarchists, thugs and paid protesters are proving the point of the millions of people who voted to MAKE AMERICA GREAT AGAIN!"

In the first weeks of the Trump administration, the factions that split over his election are deepening along the same lines. Each side seems oddly confident in its political position. Trump supporters call themselves "the silent majority," while his critics identify as the "popular vote." When I called Eleanor Smeal, a co-founder of the Feminist Majority Foundation, and asked her whether the organization had any plans to reach out to the 53 percent of white women who voted for Trump, her response was to question the margin of error in the polls. "We don't really know if we lost the majority or not, and I believe that we did not," she told me. "I think they're with us."

For now, the factions of the left seem to have found an accord. But to regain any power in Washington, they will need to sway the center too—including some of those women who voted for Trump. The white women of the left, many of whom are just now finding their footing as activists, have been eager to dissociate from that group. Mention the 53 percent, and they're quick to tell you that they're of the 47. But of all the people who marched on Washington last month, they may be among the best positioned to reach across that aisle. "I know of no other time when it would be more important," Barbara Smith, the black feminist and leftist, told me. "That's not my work to do, but somebody ought to do it."

Sexist Political Criticism Finds a New Target: Kellyanne Conway

Susan Chira

Susan Chira is assistant managing editor for news at the New York Times. *"Sexist Political Criticism Finds a New Target: Kellyanne Conway" appeared in the* New York Times *on March 5, 2017.*

What powerful political woman is mocked for her clothes, is the target of pictures on Twitter depicting her as haggard, and is routinely called a witch and a bitch? If you guessed Hillary Clinton, you're right. But if you guessed Kellyanne Conway, you're right, too.

Misogyny, it seems, remains a bipartisan exercise. Whatever legitimate criticisms can be leveled at each woman, it's striking how often that anger is expressed using the same sexist themes, from women as well as men.

Mrs. Clinton "repeats her tacky outfits," one Twitter critic sniped. The Inauguration Day outfit of Ms. Conway, a counselor to President Trump, looked like "a night terror of an android majorette."

Mrs. Clinton's hair has drawn relentless derision; one Twitter user recently asked: "Why does Kellyanne Conway always look like she's still drunk & wearing make up from last night's bender?"

And both women have been repeatedly compared to witches from *The Wizard of Oz*, most recently in pictures shared on Twitter tying Ms. Conway to the witch killed under Dorothy's house.

The two women are at opposite ideological poles, but they stir up the same lingering cultural discomfort with ambitious, assertive women.

"These sexist memes are not the purview of one party," said Karen Finney, a senior adviser to the Clinton campaign. "We fear strong women and women with power. These attacks are meant to delegitimize that power."

Ms. Conway has drawn scorn, and been disinvited from some news programs, for her references to a "Bowling Green massacre" that never took place and her defense of claims about the size of the crowd at Mr. Trump's inauguration as "alternative facts." Yet some of the criticisms have taken on a distinctly sexualized tone.

Witness the furor over her sitting on her knees on a couch in the Oval Office during a reception for presidents of historically black colleges. While she drew fire for disrespect, some of the criticisms included digs about her spreading her legs and raunchy allusions to oral sex, Monica Lewinsky, and Bill Clinton. Representative Cedric L. Richmond, Democrat of Louisiana, told a now-notorious joke that hers was a "familiar" position in the Oval Office of the 1990s, drawing a rebuke from none other than Chelsea Clinton. (Mr. Richmond apologized Sunday evening.)

A *Saturday Night Live* skit riffed on Ms. Conway as a *Fatal Attraction* stalker, breaking into the CNN correspondent Jake Tapper's house to seduce him into having her on his show.

"There seems to be great resentment of both as power hungry and wanting to control men," said Marjorie J. Spruill, the author of *Divided We Stand: The Battle Over Women's Rights and Family Values That Polarized American Politics.* "Whereas Hillary is called castrating or shrewish, Conway is often called a slut. The implication is that she is using femininity to control men."

Ms. Spruill noted that Ms. Conway had leaned back to take pictures as a favor to the participants, but that some critics had cast the pose as a sexual come-on.

Ironies abound. Ms. Conway is loathed by many Clinton aides as the architect of a presidential campaign that they felt used overtly and implicitly sexist messages. Mr. Trump repeatedly denigrated women for their appearance and, after taking office, directed his female staff members to "dress like women."

Many conservative women, from Sarah Palin to Ann Coulter, have emphasized their femininity to distance themselves from feminists, whom they accuse of hating men. In a recent interview at the Conservative Political Action Conference, Ms. Conway said she supported many feminist principles but said she would not call herself one because feminism is anti-male, pro-abortion, and identified with the left.

"I think some of the reticence that might be coming across in not a huge chorus of defense of Kellyanne Conway in the face of these sexist comments is the feeling that she doesn't have our back," said Gillian Thomas, a senior staff lawyer of the Women's Rights Project of the American Civil Liberties Union.

"It's a shame," Ms. Thomas continued. "If women were more united and speaking up at this behavior, including when it's perpetrated by the left, we'd all be a lot better off."

Ms. Conway suggested in an interview with *The Daily Caller* that there would have been more outrage at the comments if she had been a liberal woman, adding, "And it is not just if I were a liberal woman, but if I were a pro-abortion one." Ms. Conway did not respond to a message left with her assistant requesting comment for this article.

Still, Ms. Conway has spirited defenders on the right on social media who say she should be championed as an example of a groundbreaking woman in politics instead of mocked in sexist terms, and some liberal women in Facebook comments chided others for sexism.

"Ladies & Gents, I disagree with her as much as anyone," wrote someone identified as Melissa Mae. "It would be nice to see comments sticking to valid points instead of ALWAYS going after women on the basis of 'looks.'"

Mirya R. Holman, an assistant professor of political science at Tulane University who studies gender and politics, said, "This does mimic what conservative women have said in the past: 'You liberals think you're so enlightened, but we still get people saying vile things about us.'"

Jennifer Palmieri, the director of communications for the Clinton campaign, who memorably clashed with Ms. Conway at a postelection forum at Harvard, also sees echoes of the sexism that dogged her candidate in the attacks on Ms. Conway.

She said she believed Ms. Conway should be held accountable for her actions. But she noted that while Stephen K. Bannon, Mr. Trump's chief strategist, is portrayed as an "evil genius" who cannily promotes images of an America at risk from immigrants and foreign competitors, Ms. Conway is depicted as "crazy" for devising and promoting similar messages.

"What I find really disturbing is because he's a man, that's really smart and strategic," Ms. Palmieri said. "Why is there not a theory behind what Kellyanne does?"

Whether the attacks come from the right or the left, they show a persistent anger toward women who step outside conventional roles. Social media has long enabled a thriving subculture of the violent disparagement of women, such as the GamerGate threats toward those who challenged the male bastion of video games. Much as latent racism surfaced during the presidency of Barack Obama, this election exposed a vitriol toward powerful women that continues to erupt, beyond the confines of Twitter or Reddit.

"To me, the 2016 election was hopefully an opportunity to be reminded that we're not in some kind of postgender society," Professor Holman said. "There's a smaller set of acceptable behaviors for women."

Ms. Finney, a longtime Clinton aide, has watched those issues play out for more than twenty years in public life as Mrs. Clinton served as a stand-in for debates about women's roles. She said she and conservative women would sit in green rooms awaiting television appearances and trade stories about how they were attacked.

"There is this sense: 'Are you kidding me?'" she said. "'Are we going back to this?' Maybe we have to go back to go forward."

Permissions

"Hillary Clinton Has One More Badly Behaved Man Left to Vanquish" first appeared in *The Nation*. Reprinted with permission from the author, Katha Pollitt.

"What Wendy Davis Stood For" first appeared in the *New Yorker*. Reprinted with permission from Condé Nast.

"How Can We Get More Women in Elected Office? Look to New Hampshire" first appeared in *In These Times* magazine. Reprinted with permissions from Representation 20/20.

"Women Actually Do Govern Differently" first appeared in the *New York Times*. Reprinted with permission from PARS International.

"The Senate Bathroom Angle" first appeared in the *New York Times*. Reprinted with permission from PARS International.

"The Men Feminists Left Behind" first appeared in the *New York Times*. Reprinted with permission from PARS International.

"An Open Letter to White Liberal Feminists" first appeared online at the African American Intellectual History Society. Reprinted with permission from the author, LeRhonda Manigault-Bryant.

"Identity Issues Don't Distract from Economic Issues—They Are Economic Issues" first appeared in *New York* magazine. Reprinted with permission from the publication.

"Political Correctness: How the Right Invented a Phantom Enemy" first appeared in *The Guardian*. Reprinted with permission from the publication.

"Feminism Lost. Now What?" first ran in the *New York Times*. Reprinted with permission from PARS International.

"You Never Know What a Revolution Is Going to Look Like" first appeared at *London's Sunday Times*. Reprinted with permission from the author, Naomi Wolf.

"Thirteen Women Who Should Run in 2020" first appeared in the *New Yorker*. Reprinted with permission from Condé Nast.

"How a Fractious Women's Movement Came to Lead the Left" first appeared in the *New York Times*. Reprinted with permission from PARS International.

"Sexist Political Criticism Finds a New Target: Kellyanne Conway" first appeared in the *New York Times*. Reprinted with permission from PARS International.

ABOUT THE EDITOR

Diane Wachtell is the executive director of The New Press.

Celebrating 25 Years
of Independent Publishing